Contents

KV-635-328

Introduction

Straddling the equator, from which it gets its name, Ecuador is often referred to as 'a microcosm of South America' or, less scientifically, a 'boutique country'. The smallest and most accessible of the Andean countries, it is one of the most biodiverse countries on the planet, which means surprising and dramatic changes of scenery in a space smaller than Italy, around twice the size of England, or about the same size as Colorado.

Visitors can be in a humid cloudforest surrounded by birds, orchids and butterflies in the morning, and catching their breath at a volcano refuge or sunning themselves on a beach in the afternoon. Ecuador is a country with altitude, which means changes of weather, scenery, peoples and activities within just a few hours of travelling.

This is a country of superlatives, and planetary records. The volcanically active 'centre of the world' is stuffed with record numbers of orchids, birds, butterflies and trees, making it a paradise for nature lovers. It has world-class whale-watching, climbing, surfing, white-water rafting and diving, making it great for active adventurers. Colonised for a brief period by the Incas, then by the Spaniards, the country also offers culture vultures the chance to revel in well-restored Spanish colonial cities such as Quito – Ecuador's main gateway, the highest capital in South America, and the continent's largest and best-preserved

old town – and Cuenca, the 'Athens of Ecuador'. The country also has the most diverse range of indigenous cultures on the continent, accounting for around a third of the population, and is a leader in sustainable community tourism in Latin America.

The country divides into four main regions both structurally and scenically: the Andes, the Amazon, the Pacific Coast and the Galápagos Islands. The country's main tourist draw is of course the Galápagos Islands, a unique offshore archipelago justifiably referred to as 'the greatest wildlife show on earth'. Here, on wild, mostly uninhabited islands, visitors can get up close and personal with exotic seabirds and other creatures that are remarkably unafraid of humans.

Overshadowed by the jewel in its crown, Ecuador's many other attractions are often undersold. These range from working *haciendas* to colourful indigenous markets with backdrops of stunning snowcapped

TRAVELLERS

ECUADOR &
THE GALÁPAGOS ISLANDS

By
NICKI GRIHAULT

Written by Nicki Grihault
Original photography by Nicki Grihault

Published by Thomas Cook Publishing
A division of Thomas Cook Tour Operations Limited
Company registration no. 1450464 England
The Thomas Cook Business Park, Unit 9 Coningsby Road,
Peterborough PE3 8SB, United Kingdom
Email: books@thomascook.com, Tel: + 44 (0) 1733 416477
www.thomascookpublishing.com

Produced by Cambridge Publishing Management Limited
Burr Elm Court, Main Street, Caldecote CB23 7NU

ISBN: 978-1-84157-998-6

First edition © 2008 Thomas Cook Publishing
Text © Thomas Cook Publishing
Maps © Thomas Cook Publishing/PCGraphics (UK) Limited

Series Editor: Maisie Fitzpatrick
Production/DTP: Steven Collins

Printed and bound in Italy by Printer Trento

Cover photography: Front L–R: © Tiber Bognar/Alamy; © Sami Sarkis/Getty;
© Michael Simpson/Getty
Back L–R: © Keren Su/China Span/Alamy; © Pep Rolg/Alamy

The paper used for this book has been independently certified as having
been sourced from well-managed forests and recycled wood or fibre
according to the rules of the Forest Stewardship Council.
This book has been printed and bound in Italy by Printer Trento S.r.l.,
an FSC certified company for printing books on FSC mixed paper in
compliance with the chain of custody and on products labelling standards.

FSC
Mixed Sources
Product group from well-manag
forests and recycled wood or f

Cert no. CQ-COC-000012
www.fsc.org
© 1996 Forest Stewardship Coun

Andean volcanoes and crater lakes, and from river journeys through Amazon jungle where pumas and jaguars still roam, to long, deserted beaches which offer some of the world's best whale-watching. And don't forget the possibilities for visiting fascinating indigenous tribes that still inhabit the jungles, or exploring the remains of pre-Columbian cultures.

Most visitors head to the Galápagos Islands, spending a couple of days in and around the gateways of Quito or Guayaquil on the way in or out. Add-ons typically include the Andes between Otavalo in the north as far as Cuenca in the south, or one of a handful of jungle lodges in the Amazon. Much of the country is off the beaten track. With its overwhelming diversity, Ecuador is truly an adventure of the senses. Wherever you go, you'll encounter Ecuador's unsung delight – its people, known as some of the friendliest in the region, and courteous, genuine and helpful.

Introduction

The countryside of Ecuador is ideal for adventurous walks

The land

Situated in the northwest of South America, Ecuador is bounded on the west by the Pacific Ocean, on the north by Colombia, and on the east and south by Peru. Its four main geographical regions are subdivided into 22 provinces, and 33 state-protected reserves cover 18 per cent of the country's area. The three mainland regions run lengthways along the country, side by side. The Andes or 'Sierra' is the heart and spine of Ecuador, and the region contains half the country's population in cities such as Quito and Cuenca.

Bounded by the eastern and western mountain chains, the Panamericana highway cuts through a fertile farming region of working haciendas, cut-flower plantations and Indian villages where alpacas and llamas roam, surrounded

Alpacas are a frequent sight across the land

by over 30, mostly snowcapped volcanoes, including the highest active volcano in the world, Cotopaxi, at 5,897m (19,347ft).

To the west, 2,237km (1,390 miles) of Pacific Coast or 'Costa' is dotted with fishing villages and fringed by dry tropical forest and mangrove. Inland are banana, cacao, palm and coffee plantations and, along with a quarter of the country's landmass, this area encompasses the populous port city of Guayaquil.

To the east, the Andean peaks give way to the Amazon jungle or 'Oriente', a huge stretch of forest criss-crossed by rivers, with the 855km-long (530-mile) Río Napo the main highway.

Some 1,000km (620 miles) west off the Ecuadorian coast are the Galápagos Islands, the peaks of underwater or 'submarine' volcanoes. Comprising 13 main islands and over 40 small islands and islets, they're famed for their unique populations of extraordinary and fearless wildlife.

Legend:
- City
- Large Town
- Small Town
- POI
- Main Road
- Minor Road
- Airport
- Railway

0   100km
0   50 miles

Naya

Cali

Neiva

Mosquera

Popayán

Garzón

Pacific Ocean

Tumaco

Pasto

Florencia

Esmeraldas

Tachina

Ipiales

COLOMBIA

Tulcán

Ibarra   35

Equator

Santo Domingo de los Colorados

Mariscal Sucre International

Otavalo

Nueva Loja

QUITO

Volcán Cotopaxi ▲ 5897

Providencia

30

35

Napo

Latacunga

Cotopaxi International

Tena

Manta

Eloy Alfaro

Portoviejo

Ambato

ECUADOR

9

Babahoyo

Riobamba

Conambo

Guayaquil

Simón Bolívar

60

Alausí

Macas

La Libertad

Cuenca

PERU

Andoas Nuevo

Machala

60

28 de Mayo

Tumbes

35

Darwin (Abingdon)

Pinta (Abingdon)

Wolf

Marchena (Bindloe)

Genovesa (Tower)

0   60km
0   30 miles

Equator

92

Santiago (James/San Salvador)

Pacific Ocean

Alamor

Loja

Zamora

Fernandina (Narborough)

Santa Cruz (Indefatigable)

San Cristóbal (Chatham)

Sullana

Vilcabamba

Isabela (Albemarle)

Santa Fé

Galápagos

Ayabaca

Zumba

Piura

Floreana (Santa María/Charles)

Española (Hood)

Olmos

Chachapoyas

Moyobamba

1A

N

Chiclayo

Tarapoto

Cajamarca

Balsas

The natural world

Ecuador is the most biodiverse country on the planet for its size, and with UNESCO World Heritage Sites, marine reserves and geobotanical reserves, it's a paradise for nature lovers. Its 46 different ecosystems are home to a mind-boggling 9.2 species to every 1sq km (⅓sq mile) – and the country has 283,561 of them (109,484sq miles). This translates to over 1,600 bird species (a sixth of the world's total), 250 mammals, 358 amphibians and 345 reptiles, 4,500 butterflies and millions of unidentified insects. It's also home to 10 per cent (or 20,000) of the world's plant species, including over 4,000 orchids – a figure unmatched by anywhere else on earth. Not only is the country considered one of the most species-rich on the planet, it also has one of the highest levels of endemic species. Its most extraordinary and unique ecosystem is the Galápagos Islands, whose wildlife inspired Darwin's theory of evolution.

The country is located on zero latitude, which affects many of Ecuador's geographic features and means that flowers, for example, are in bloom year-round. Altitude informs over 24 natural tropical life zones including cloudforest, páramo, rainforest, coastal dry forest and mangrove swamps.

Thick fog from the sea in the afternoons cloaks Andean slopes between 900m and 2,500m (2,950ft and 8,200ft), creating **cloudforest** (subtropical rainforest). Mist lingers in the branches of stunted trees in these fairy-like, waterfall-filled kingdoms dripping with rootless epiphytes or 'air plants' such as orchids (around 40 per cent endemic) and bromeliads, which live on air moisture. Underneath, colourful frogs, butterflies and birds abound – in particular hummingbirds – and spectacled bears and pumas roam.

The *páramo*, found between 3,200m and 4,200m (10,500ft and 13,800ft), covers around 10 per cent

PROTECTING THE FOREST

Ecuador is home to some of the most biodiverse and critically endangered forest on earth, and **Rainforest Concern** (*www.rainforestconcern.org*) is an important group that supports community-run eco-lodges and areas of exceptional biodiversity here. Two lodges supported by Rainforest Concern are Santa Lucia (*www.santaluciaecuador.com*), an award-winning eco-lodge in the Northwestern Andean cloudforest (*p161*), and Yachana, an educational lodge in the Northern Amazon (*see p167*).

Ecuador's forests are home to a mesmerising diversity of wildlife

of Ecuador. A tropical wet alpine habitat, its almost treeless landscape of moorland or tundra, comprised of hard grasses, bromeliads and ferns, is rich in wildflowers and medicinal plants. Like a saturated sponge, it provides the cities with water.

The Amazon **rainforest** is a non-seasonal forest with constant and abundant rainfall. Taller trees form a canopy that blocks out sunlight, so only shade-dwellers such as palms and ferns live underneath, creating a jungle pharmacy that provides many of the world's medicinal plants. Flooded forest provides nutrients and diverse marine life, and being hilly – ranging between 40m and 1,000m (130ft and 3,280ft) – and criss-crossed by hundreds of rivers, the rainforest has a plethora of waterfalls, including San Rafael, the highest in

Ecuador. The animals living here are some of the most exotic on earth and range from the tiniest pygmy monkey to the legendary jaguar.

On the other hand, **tropical dry forest**, found at the low altitudes of the Galápagos and the Pacific Coast, is characterised by hardy cacti such as opuntia, lichens that live on air moisture, and ghostly white *palo santo* trees, which smell of incense in the sun's heat. The most famous tree found here, however, is the dramatic *ceiba* or kapok tree.

Also occurring at low altitudes, although many have been destroyed to make way for shrimp farms, **mangrove swamps** are essential breeding grounds for fish and lie along the edges of the Galápagos Islands and on parts of the Pacific Coast.

History

10,000 BC The first hunter-gatherers and fishing communities arrive at the coast. They comprise the pre-Inca cultures central to Ecuadorian identity. Other early Ecuadorians came from Brazil, but the coastal communities are believed to have been descendants of Asian nomads who crossed the Bering Strait.

4000–500 BC During this formative period the first settled culture, the Valdivia, produces South America's first ceramics, the Chorrea are influential, and Machalilla culture is known for skull-flattening practices.

700–600 BC Societies become organised and cultures such as the Bahía expand maritime trade across the continent. La Tolita advances metallurgy and art.

800 BC–AD 1500 Hierarchical societies develop such as the coastal Manteños, the highland Quitu-Caras and the southern Cañari.

AD 1460 Incas move north from Peru, conquer the natives and introduce the potato and their Kichwa language, reaching Quito in 1492. The last Inca king, Atahualpa, is the son of the Inca leader and a Cañari princess.

1526–34 After only 70 years, the Inca empire, weakened by civil war, is overthrown by the Spanish conquistadors, led by Francisco Pizarro. His lieutenant, Sebastián de Benalcázar, captures Quito in 1534, bringing Ecuador under tough Spanish colonial rule for 300 years, imposing Catholicism, law and custom, language and disease on the indigenous Indians. The Spanish 'employ' them as indentured labourers on vast estates or *haciendas*, producing everything from bulls to textiles. In the first six months after the conquest, they melt down and ship 80,000 tonnes (88,180 tons) of gold and 120,000 tonnes (132,300 tons) of silver to Europe.

1541	Francisco de Orellana discovers the Amazon.
1660–1760	The Escuela Quiteña (Quito School) flourishes to produce some of the world's best religious art.
1736	A French-led expedition locates the equator.
1809–10	*Criollos* (Spanish people born in the colonies), resentful of high taxes, push for independence. Independence fighters are quashed.
1822–30	Marshal Sucre defeats Spaniards in the Battle of Pichincha. Simón de Bolívar incorporates Ecuador into Gran Colombia. Ecuador becomes an independent republic in 1830.
1832–5	Ecuador annexes the Galápagos Islands and Charles Darwin arrives on the *Beagle*.
1880	British climber Edward Whymper is the first to ascend Chimborazo, Ecuador's highest volcano.
1941–8	A border dispute with Peru means a loss of Amazon territory, but the subsequent banana boom sees Ecuador emerge as the world's leading exporter of the fruit.
1964	Land reform returns land to the indigenous population.
1970s	Ecuador becomes one of the largest oil exporters in the world, which leads to a return to democracy.
1998	Ecuador and Peru sign a peace treaty, ending their half-century border dispute.
1999	Pichincha and Tungurahua volcanoes erupt, spewing ash over Quito and forcing the evacuation of Baños.
2000–2007	In an effort to stabilise the economy, Ecuador adopts the US dollar as its national currency. After political instability caused by five presidents in as many years, the left-wing Rafael Correa is appointed in 2007.
2008	Quito marks 30 years as first World Heritage City.
2009	The 200th anniversary of the 'First Cry of Liberty' in the war of Independence from Spain.

Politics

Having had five presidents in the 12 years running up to the election of Rafael Correa in 2007, Ecuador's dizzying political instability has often grabbed headlines rather than the fact that Ecuador has lower corruption levels than most Latin American countries; indeed, people here protest until they oust lousy politicians out of office. Despite a history of military takeovers, firebrand politicians and jail dramas, politics here is tame compared to the bloodshed and brutality seen in much of the continent.

It wasn't indigenous Indians, now accounting for 30–40 per cent of the vote, who protested their way to independence, but the *Criollos*, Spanish descendants disgruntled at the high taxes demanded by the crown. The place to get an insight into the history of politics, then, is the *haciendas*, which are all owned by notable political families.

Traditionally, Ecuadorian politics have been a tug of war between coastal liberals and the conservative highlanders. However, the campaign of the current president – leftist, neo-liberal, charismatic Rafael Correa – against millionaire banana king Álvaro Noboa was dubbed Marx against Markets.

POLITICAL PASSION

As Indians have 40 per cent of the vote, the most humble dwellings and villages, and even boats in the Galápagos, get political and have posters and slogans supporting one president or another. With five having been in office over the last 12 years, there's a variety of names!

Although it was once a banana republic, oil now turns the wheels of the Ecuadorian economy, followed by money sent from Ecuadorians living overseas – post 'dollarisation' in 2000. Tourism is the third most important income for the country, followed by bananas, roses, tuna and shrimp exports.

Shaping the country

To find the names of Ecuador's political figures, as well as key historical dates, just look at the names of its streets. The conservative Catholic dictator Gabriel García Moreno came to power in 1861. He built the important Panamericana highway before being assassinated on the steps of the presidential palace in 1875, taking his last breath in the cathedral opposite. To hear about the less conservative side of his life – a mistress and possible wife-poisoning – visit Hacienda Guachalá.

Liberal president Eloy Alfaro (1897–1901 and 1906–11) attempted to loosen the Church's hold on the state before meeting a nasty end at the hands of a conservative mob. His greatest achievement was perhaps the completion of the trans-Andean railway using his Western contacts. A new political museum is dedicated to Alfaro in his birthplace of Montecristi. President Correa is a relative.

The Plaza-Lasso family is one of the most politically distinguished in Ecuador. General Leónidas Plaza Gutiérrez (1901–5 and 1912–16) was the leader of the liberal revolution, giving the land to the state, the vote to women and today's constitution to the country. His son, the much-loved Galo Plaza Lasso (1948–52), often referred to as Ecuador's last decent president, balanced the extremes of his liberal and conservative parents and, seeing a revolution coming, introduced land reform.

As for Correa, well-meaning if a little hot-headed and contradictory, his efforts to stand up to oil exploitation (and risk US ire) have been followed by the bold step of rewriting the constitution. Ecuador's landowners and the US wait with bated breath, but Correa's leftist policies may be tempered after he witnessed his key ally, President Hugo Chávez of Venezuela, suffer a political blow in 2007. And, for now, the country is enjoying a period of relative stability.

Politics

A monument to Abdón Calderón, who fought for independence, adorns a square in Cuenca

Culture

Ecuador's biological diversity is echoed in its culture. Although most of the population is mestizo (of mixed racial ancestry, mainly Indian and Spanish extraction), it includes people from 27 different ethnic backgrounds, including 13 indigenous groups, giving rise to a wide range of cultural expression through art, architecture, music, dance and many fiestas (see pp18–19). Many of Ecuador's artists have been political, fighting against injustice, exploring key issues and calling for change.

Ecuador has more than enough for culture vultures in cities that are UNESCO World Heritage Sites. Works from the famous art movement Escuela Quiteña (the Quito School of Art), with their indigenous interpretation of Catholic themes (*see p26*), were exported throughout the continent in Spanish colonial times. Also famous is the leading painter of the 20th-century indigenous artistic movement, Oswaldo Guayasamín, whose works explore the indigenous struggle. Both are found in the country's capital, itself the largest and best-preserved old town in South America. As if this weren't enough, dazzling churches, wonderful religious sculptures and contemporary artisans await in Ecuador's cultural mecca, the 'City of Churches', Cuenca.

Cuenca also lies near the country's best Inca ruins. It was the sun overhead at the equator that drew the 'sons of the sun', the Incas, to Ecuador, for a brief 72-year rule. They may have left their language, Kichwa, and some culture in the form of men sporting Inca ponytails, but a more pervasive effect is felt from pre-Columbian cultures such as La Tolita, whose artistic influence stretched across the continent. Original pre-Columbian art seen in museums country-wide, and even decorating the walls of *haciendas*, far outweighs Incan artefacts and is uniquely Ecuadorian.

Textiles were important historically and are still woven using centuries-old methods in villages of the Andes today (*see p37*), traditions that adapted to the waves of colonisation, using alpaca, introduced by the Incas, and sheeps' wool, brought by the Spanish. In colonial times, Ecuadorian textiles were imported all over the empire and, in later years, even as far as the USA. A more contemporary expression of indigenous art has sprung up in the village of Tigua, with a Naïf style of painting on animal hides, exploring typical Andean themes from fiestas to shamans and animal-herding.

A work of art from Cotacachi in the Otavalo region highlights the suffering of indigenous people

Visitors will also recognise the haunting traditional Andean folk music – 'El Cóndor Pasa' is as famous as 'Guantanamera' – played on Ecuadorian panpipes (*rondador*), accompanied by guitar, flutes and the *guarumo* horn. Such music is often played in *haciendas* or tourist establishments but is best heard at *peñas* or folk music clubs (*see Directory, p158*). Outside of fiestas, diverse and elaborate regional folk dances centred around themes such as the harvest or hunting can be seen performed at Jacchigua in Quito (*see Directory, pp158–9*).

Also in the Andes is living history of a different kind, found in the *haciendas*, colonial mansions and land given by the Spanish crown, which have nurtured presidents and revolutionary heroes.

Early writers, such as Eugenio Espejo and José Joaquín de Olmedo, were involved in the independence movement and set the tone for most of Ecuador's famous literature, which still today explores political themes, with many works focusing on the pain and suffering of indigenous people.

Ecuador has had some international cinematic success, too, with films also focusing on themes such as indigenous culture, corruption and the underworld.

Indigenous peoples of Ecuador

With 13 distinct indigenous groups, Ecuador's cultural diversity is unmatched by other Andean countries. The most prominent – descended from Asians who crossed the Bering Strait between 40,000 and 20,000 BC – are the agricultural Kichwa-speaking people in the Andes, who breed guinea pigs to roast at fiestas, whose native houses are thatch domes with wooden doors, and whose women's traditional dress consists of beautifully embroidered blouses, with gold-coloured bead necklaces and shawls (ponchos for men), inspired by the ancient fashions of Spanish nobility. Topped off by stylish hats (from Italy), dress varies between villages, incorporating the colour and patterns used to identify workers on different *haciendas*.

The most distinctive Andean peoples were forcibly relocated from Bolivia and Peru by the Incas under the *mitimae* or 'spreading' system designed to quell uprisings and colonise the continent. The Otavaleños were sent north, the Salasacas to the centre and the Saraguros south. The Otavaleños are Ecuador's most famous and prosperous indigenous group, exporting their Andean music, handicrafts and textiles. Perhaps the Colorados, near Quito, who traditionally dye their hair red with *achiote*, are the most dramatic. Jacchigua (*see pp158–9*) in Quito showcases the great variety of Andean costumes, music and dances.

The ancestors of the warrior-like hunters called Huaorani, their bowl-like haircuts thought to be inspired by the Spanish soldiers' military helmets, and the Shuar (part of Aschuar), who once shrunk the heads of enemies, came upriver from Brazil. To the north, Cofán men wear dramatic parrot-feather headdresses (once for ceremonies, now for tourists) and speak a language of the Central American Chibchan family. And vibrant Afro-Ecuadorians in Esmeraldas on the northwest coast are famous for music and dance, and bamboo houses on stilts are traditional here.

MINGA

If you see people toiling together, you may be witnessing a *minga* (community work), an extension of a help-thy-neighbour attitude which continues in indigenous communities today.

Plight of the Indians

When Columbus discovered America, he wasn't clear whether the natives were to be considered human beings. The Indian population was almost decimated by brutal working conditions, first as slaves to the Incas, who wiped out indigenous languages, and then as indentured labourers to the Spaniards on their *haciendas*. It was only the land reform in 1964 that gave each family land for sustainable agriculture. However, not all of this is workable, which has caused migration to the cities and further poverty, or even a return to working on the *haciendas*.

Amazon utopia was destroyed (only 50 years ago for some communities) by missionaries, paving the way for destruction by oil and timber companies and reducing numbers through disease, displacement and colonisation (*see pp86–7*).

Although Ecuador treats its Indians better than many Latin American countries, they experience problems in common with disenfranchised indigenous groups, such as alcoholism, domestic violence, malnutrition and apathy caused by charitable handouts.

Experiencing indigenous culture

The best way to meet and help indigenous people is by visiting an established and successful community project, such as one of those listed in 'Ecotourism in Ecuador' (*see pp82–3*), but much can also be learned from visiting some of the excellent museums and cultural exhibits on offer. Some of the best are the Museo de la Ciudad (*see p31*) and the Museo Mindalae (*see p33*) in Quito, the Posada de Estación in Urbina (*see p164*) and the Museo de las Culturas Aborígenes in Cuenca (*see p68*).

A cultural show at Mitad del Mundo

Festivals and events

Ecuadorians love a party and there are always plenty of excuses for a fiesta, from Columbus' arrival and the liberation of the country to religious or indigenous festivals or, often, a mix of the two. Each town honours its protector and history and this can sometimes culminate in month-long celebrations. As important, vibrant and colourful expressions of Ecuadorian culture and identity, fiestas are a worthwhile focus for your trip, although be sure to book hotels well in advance.

End February/early March
Carnival
Celebrated with lavish parades and water fights throughout the country, carnival is combined with an elegant **Fiesta de las Frutas y las Flores** (Festival of Fruits and Flowers) in Ambato, and in Guaranda is celebrated with potent *aguardiente*.
Countrywide, the week before Lent

March/April
Semana Santa (Holy Week)
The biggest Easter procession is in Quito's old town on Good Friday. Fanesca (a traditional grain stew) is eaten everywhere. Ecuadorians, however, traditionally head to the beach.
Countrywide, around Easter

June
Inti Raymi (Festival of the Sun)
The indigenous festival, derived from ancient practices, celebrates the summer solstice.
Sacred sites in Otavalo and Northern Andes, 21 June

**San Juan Bautista
(St John the Baptist's Day)**
This day is celebrated with ancient practices of bathing, dancing in traditional costume and ritual fighting!
Otavalo and surrounds, 24 June

Corpus Christi (Body of Christ)
Harvest festival with parades and colourful masked dancers in Pujili and Salasaca.
Central and Southern Andes, 9th Thursday after Easter

Festival-goer in Cayambe

July
**Natalicio Simón Bolívar
(Simón Bolívar's birthday)**
A patriotic celebration of South
America's liberator, with colourful
parades, dancing and traditional
costumes.
Countrywide, 24 July

August
**Fiesta Virgen El Cisne
(Festival of the El Cisne Virgin)**
The cult formed around this painted
wooden virgin comes into full
expression as thousands of pilgrims
parade it the 70km (44 miles) from
El Cisne village to Loja's cathedral.
Loja province, 15 August

September
Fiesta de la Jora (Corn Festival)
Alcoholic *chicha* made from corn is
offered in praise of the sun god and a
Paseo del Chagra is a chance to see
cowboys' mastery of their horses.
The Andes, Cotacachi, autumn equinox

La Mama Negra (The Black Mother)
Ecuador's most colourful and famous
festival parades the Virgen de la Merced
to a nearby hill, while in the streets
there are dancing, floats and fireworks,
and a man symbolically dressed as a
black woman.
Latacunga, 24 September

Fiesta del Yamor
The autumn equinox and Colla Raimi
(Festival of the Moon) are celebrated
with parties accompanied by *yamor*
(a non-alcoholic corn drink).
Imbabura province, 1–15 September

November
**El Día de los Muertos
(Day of the Dead)**
Indigenous people lay fruit and flowers
in cemeteries in order to honour their
ancestors, and prepare a special fruit
juice, *Colada morada*, with *guaguas de
pan*, bread figures.
*Countrywide, particularly the Andes,
2 November*

Independence Day
This three-day party is Cuenca's biggest
celebration, with events all over town.
Cuenca, 3 November

December
Founder's Day
Bullfighting and riding on open-sided
chivas with a live band and booze is
traditional. A lively blur of parades,
fireworks and dancing.
Quito, 6 December

Nochebuena (Christmas Eve)
Cuenca's traditional religious Christmas
parade is spectacular.
Cuenca, 24 December

Nochevieja (New Year's Eve)
Ecuador celebrates by burning
life-size puppets and effigies
associated with the old year in the
streets at midnight.
Countrywide, 28–31 December

Highlights

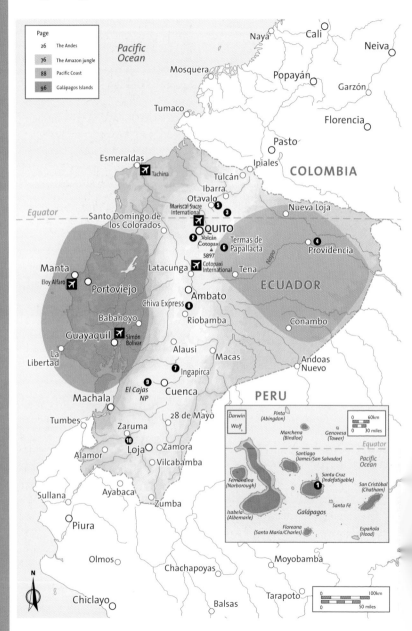

Pacific Ocean

Naya   Cali   Neiva

Mosquera   Popayán   Garzón

Tumaco   Florencia

Pasto

Esmeraldas   Ipiales

Tachina   Tulcán   COLOMBIA

Ibarra

Otavalo

Mariscal Sucre International

Equator

Santo Domingo de los Colorados   Nueva Loja

QUITO

Volcán Cotopaxi 5897   Termas de Papallacta   Providencia

Manta   Latacunga   Cotopaxi International   Tena   ECUADOR

Eloy Alfaro

Portoviejo

Chiva Express   Ambato

Babahoyo   Riobamba

Guayaquil   Simón Bolívar   Conambo

La Libertad   Alausí   Macas

Ingapirca   Andoas Nuevo

El Cajas NP   Cuenca   PERU

Machala

Tumbes   28 de Mayo

Zaruma

Loja   Zamora

Alamor   Vilcabamba

Sullana   Ayabaca   Zumba

Piura

Olmos   Chachapoyas   Moyobamba

Chiclayo   Balsas   Tarapoto

Darwin   Pinta (Abingdon)

Wolf   Marchena (Bindloe)   Genovesa (Tower)

Equator

Santiago (James/San Salvador)

Pacific Ocean

Fernandina (Narborough)   Santa Cruz (Indefatigable)   San Cristóbal (Chatham)

Santa Fé

Isabela (Albemarle)   Galápagos

Floreana (Santa María/Charles)   Española (Hood)

0   60km
0   30 miles

0   100km
0   50 miles

N

❶ **Cruising the Galápagos Islands** visiting fearless and unusual creatures such as blue-footed boobies and giant tortoises on wild and often uninhabited islands… a once-in-a-lifetime experience (*see pp98–9*).

❷ **Walking around Quito's old town**, the largest and best-preserved in South America, with stunning colonial architecture, imposing plazas, impressive museums and gilded churches filled with unique religious art (*see pp34–5*).

❸ **Riding horses bred at Hacienda Zuleta**, run by the descendants of past presidents, on a trail past ancient burial sites to a condor rehabilitation project (*see pp40 and 50–51*).

❹ **Staying at Napo Wildlife Center** deep in the Amazon jungle. These romantic thatched cabanas, set on a lake, can only be reached by dugout canoe (*see pp78–9*).

The stables at Hacienda Zuleta

❺ **Browsing through Otavalo's Saturday market**, the largest in South America, selling everything from hooded alpaca jumpers to prize pigs, and as good for people-watching as for souvenir shopping (*see p38*).

❻ **Relaxing in the hot springs at Papallacta**, where bathing in steaming pools surrounded by mountains and fresh air and being pampered in the spa is the order of the day (*see pp80–81*).

❼ **Wandering the ruins of Ingapirca**, the most important Inca site in the country, set atmospherically atop a hill in Cañari territory in the south (*see p69*).

❽ **Taking the Chiva Express** through the 'Avenue of the Volcanoes' to Cotopaxi National Park and beyond, picking it up again at Riobamba to ride to the Devil's Nose (*see pp52–3*).

❾ **Exploring Cajas National Park**, a well-run park of pristine lakes and hillsides that look like the Scottish highlands, near Cuenca (*see p70*).

❿ **Visiting the gold-mining magnet of Zaruma**, a remote town in the hills with beautiful colonial buildings that give the place an old-time charm, and the best coffee in Ecuador (*see pp118–19*).

Suggested itineraries

Ecuador is a compact country, with attractions all no more than a day's travel from the capital and easily accessible by plane or road. It offers something for every kind of traveller, for every budget and every age, but it is particularly good for wildlife and nature lovers and adventurous and active travellers. Most visitors head to the Galápagos Islands, tagging on a couple of days in the gateways of Quito or Guayaquil.

Those who venture into mainland Ecuador usually include a visit to the Andes – Otavalo in the north as far as Cuenca in the south – or a stay in an Amazon lodge. For most, this is exotic enough, so for those who want to 'get away from it all', the rest of the country is your oyster.

Long weekend

Culture vultures and romantics will enjoy 48 hours in the Centro Histórico, the largest and best-preserved colonial city in Latin America, in the high-altitude capital Quito. The city is the main international flight gateway as well as a hotspot for gourmet restaurants and bohemian nightlife. Visitors are spoilt for choice of attractions to visit nearby. A couple of hours' drive away by bus, tour or car transfer are Otavalo (with South America's largest Saturday market), world-class birding in the cloudforests of Mindo, sumptuous *haciendas*, Cotopaxi (the most picturesque and accessible of Ecuador's volcanoes) and, on the

The historic centre of Quito is a good base for exploring the surrounding region

The lodges of Papallacta provide a welcome break from the bustling capital

Amazon's edge, hot springs in lush mountain scenery at Papallacta and waterfalls at lively Baños.

One week

Four nights/five days is the minimum for a Galápagos cruise, and, as the flight and transfers take around a day either side, it's a good idea to fly in and out of Guayaquil, to avoid acclimatisation problems and squeeze in an afternoon's sightseeing and souvenir shopping there. A land-based Galápagos tour – the Finch Bay Hotel offers day trips to islands – may allow for a couple of days in Quito and, acclimatisation willing, a choice of excursions. Alternatively, three nights/four days at an Amazon lodge or on a riverboat instead will leave you with almost half your time free to explore.

Two weeks

Fly into Quito for a week-long cruise to the farther-flung islands in the Galápagos and, for the greatest diversity, spend the second week in an Amazon lodge or on a riverboat before exploring the capital. Alternatively, the second week could be spent taking day trips from the capital (*see opposite*) to get a taste of the country. If you like to see a lot in a short time, you can choose a shorter Galápagos cruise or land-based tour, which will give you time to squeeze in the three- to five-day *Chiva Express* journey south through the Andes, taking in Cotopaxi National Park, the Devil's Nose and Cuenca, El Cajas National Park and the Inca ruins at Ingapirca. An off-the-beaten-track itinerary could include a walking tour of Isabela or Isla de la Plata instead of

Traditionally decorated building in Zaruma

whether it be horse riding between *haciendas*, whale-watching on the coast (in season just a quick flight hop from Manta), birding, scuba diving, white-water rafting, mountain biking, climbing or perhaps trekking Ecuador's Inca Trail.

Longer visits

A month in Ecuador allows you to taste most of the country, taking in the main sites and more, and dipping into other areas depending on interest and season: you can catch a fiesta, climb a volcano, learn Spanish in Quito, or simply head for the beach (an easy flight hop from Quito to Manta). Then there's always visiting the many wonderful national parks, checking out the secrets of longevity in Vilcabamba, visiting quaint Zaruma and lush Zamora (*see pp118–19*), or spending days exploring northern attractions from the comfortable base of a *hacienda*.

the Galápagos, and a flight to Cuenca and El Cajas or a trip north to the Quilotoa Loop or an indigenous homestay, or to a community cloudforest project in the northeastern Andes. One week or even two can be spent indulging special interests,

THEMED DRIVES OR RUTAS

Themed routes can be taken from Quito (maps available from the **Quito Visitors Bureau** – in Spanish). For keen birders, the **Ecoruta** from Quito to Mindo is a good choice, best tackled by mountain bike on day tours (*see 'The Biking Dutchman', p159*), starting from the slopes of Pichincha volcano. The **Ruta Quito-Tulipe**, an archaeological route to the ruins of Tulipe, takes in an orchid farm, indigenous cloudforest project and the Mitad del Mundo monument. The off-the-beaten-track **Ruta del Agua** goes to the Amazon's edge, taking in Termas de Papallacta and going via Baeza to San Rafael Waterfall.

Ecuador's most popular scenic drive is the **Ruta del Sol** (*see pp94–5*), starting from Guayaquil and hugging the coast to Manabi province. It takes in small fishing villages, Panama hat country and beaches, pre-Columbian ruins and seasonal whale-watching and bird-spotting in the Machalilla National Park.

Intriguing routes being developed include the **Ruta del Cacao** – Ecuador produces the best cocoa in the world – the **Ruta de la Canela** from Baños to Puyo, tracing the conquistadors' search for cinnamon, and the **Ruta del Spondylus**, providing an insight into pre-Columbian societies on the old trading route.

blue-footed booby nesting on Isla de la Plata

The Andes

The world's youngest – and South America's longest – mountain chain, the Andes extends 7,245km (4,500 miles) from Colombia to Patagonia. It runs north to south as Ecuador's spine, linking the country's most beautiful cities. Nestled between western and eastern ranges are fertile valleys fed by the ashes of volcanic eruptions and scattered with indigenous villages and elegant haciendas. Surrounded by around 30 volcanic peaks, many still active, this region combines adventure and nature with luxury and culture.

QUITO

At 2,850m (9,350ft), Ecuador's capital, Quito, is the second-highest city in the world and the first to be declared a UNESCO World Heritage Site – in 1978. Shaped like a worm, it's cradled in a narrow Andean valley, under the shadow of the active Pichincha volcano (4,737m/15,540ft). Quito evolved from a *tianguez*, or trading place, to become the administrative centre of the Incas before being 'founded' as San Francisco de Quito in 1534. Made Ecuador's capital at independence in 1830, it is now home to 1.5 million people and divides into a Centro Histórico and New Town. All roads lead to and from Quito, making it the best base from which to explore the country.

Centro Histórico

Once known as the 'Florence of the New World', Quito's Centro Histórico, or historical centre, is the largest and best preserved in Latin America. Its 320ha (800 acres) are home to a mind-boggling 40 churches and chapels, 16 convents and monasteries, 17 plazas, 12 museums and 5 centuries of art. Just as striking are the many indigenous people, distinct in their colourful Andean dress. Set out on a grid pattern, this part of the city is easy to explore on foot, with tweeting birds the cross signal at traffic lights.

ESCUELA QUITEÑA (THE QUITO SCHOOL OF ART)

Catholic religious art attained a distinctive style in the hands of indigenous sculptors and painters during the 17th and 18th centuries. Christian themes were expressed in detail (sculptures of saints were given real hair and glass eyes) and with disturbing realism (a bloody Christ hanging on a cross, his face contorted in agony). Local traditions crept in, with Christ eating *cuy* ('guinea pig') in paintings, and gargoyles of condors or tortoises included. See examples in Quito's churches; the Iglesia de San Francisco and La Compañía, for instance, feature celebrated artists such as Bernardo de Legarda, Caspicara and Miguel de Santiago.

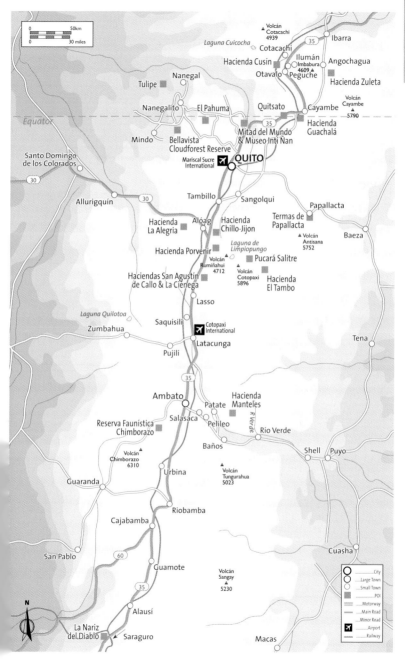

The magnificent Jesuit church of La Compañía took 163 years to complete

Once a no-go area, the centre has had a facelift, with colonial buildings restored and shopping centres, restaurants, hotels and security police installed. Street vendors still offer everything from eggs to Amazonian 'dragon's blood'. Look out for colourful events in the plazas on Sundays, when the streets are closed to traffic and it's time to breathe easy.

Leaflets with themed walking tours, such as 'Discovering the Seven Crosses' (along Calle García Moreno from the basilica to Panchillo Hill), are available from the **Quito Visitors Centre** (*Palacio Municipal, Plaza de la Independencia. Tel. (02) 228 1904. Open: Mon–Fri 9am–8pm, Sat 10am–8pm, Sun 10am–4pm*). Guided tours can also be arranged here.

Free two-hour taster tours are offered by English-speaking Metropolitan

Police guides, which leave for the Centro Histórico on demand. Some also take in modern Quito and Mitad del Mundo.

The **Tourist Information Centre** is on Plaza Gabriela Mistral (*Reina Victoria & Cordero, Mariscal. Tel: (02) 257 0786. Open: Mon–Sat 9am–5pm*).

La Basílica

This imposing 19th-century Gothic church is Ecuador's largest. See animals from the Galápagos among the many rooftop gargoyles. Inside, austere stone is enlivened by the splash of stained-glass windows. The church towers – still a neck-cricking 78m (256ft) – are shorter than planned due to earthquake risk. Climb up vertiginous open-air ladders for a stupendous view of the clock towers framing the winged, silver Virgen de

Quito atop Panchillo Hill, or catch the view through a telescope on the third floor.

If you are sufficiently inspired by the art you see, **René Toapanta Rivera** offers inexpensive drop-in painting lessons (*9am–5pm*) next to the café in the basilica's square.
Corner of Carchi & Venezuela. Tel: (02) 228 6063. Open: Mon–Sun 9am–5pm. Mass: Sun 7am & 1pm, Mon–Sat 7am & 9pm. Free admission, but charge for tower (pay at the ticket booth on the square's left side).

Casa Museo María Augusta Urrutia

Used by film-makers to represent colonial times, this 19th-century house and its interior give a glimpse into a bygone upper-class life. Among the art treasures are archangels by Mideros in the bedroom and a hand-painted bathroom window. Gilded chairs beside lacy curtains add whimsy, as do ivory inlaid cabinets from Quito.
García Moreno N2-60, between Sucre & Bolívar. Tel: (02) 238 0103/0107. www.fmdj.org. Open: Tue–Sat 10am–6pm, Sun 9.30am–5.30pm. Admission charge, but no English-speaking guides.

THE SOUND OF MUSIC

The busker (*see photo*) playing a guitar stuck with bank notes opposite La Compañía is retired revolutionary Miguel Monterrey, jailed repeatedly for singing anti-government songs.

La Compañía de Jesús

Begun in 1605, this Jesuit church took 163 years to build. Cherubs, volcanic stone lacework and twisted columns grace the Baroque façade, the most glorious in South America. Inside is a church dripping in over 50 tonnes of gold. Eyes go to the altar (a dizzying mass of sculpted gold), the Moorish-style vaulted ceiling, the deep pink and gold columns and octagonal dome – and jaws go to the floor.
Corner of García Moreno & Sucre. Mass: daily 8am & 6pm. Admission charge.

Convento de Santa Catalina

In the only working convent open to visitors here, cloistered nuns sell homemade fruit cordial, creams and candles through a wooden hatch that renders them faceless. But peek through a grille to see them silently departing for prayers from bedrooms named after

A former revolutionary busks opposite La Compañía

saints. Rumour has it that a dog named Beethoven rings the church bell.

Corner of Espejo 779 & Juan José Flores. Tel: (02) 295 9632. Museum open: Mon–Sat 8.30am–5.15pm. Admission charge.

Iglesia de la Merced

This square, plain 18th-century church has the city's highest bell tower. Inside are ornate white plaster reliefs on strawberry-pink and neon-lit sculptures of a bleeding Jesus. Its main altarpiece was carved by Bernardo de Legarda.

Corner of Chile & Cuenca. Open: 7am–noon & 2–7pm. Free admission.

Plaza de la Independencia

The heart of the old town for Quiteños, demonstrations, religious processions and rousing concerts are held in this plaza centred around a statue celebrating independence. Flanked by blue and gold uniformed guards, the arches below the sombre **Palacio del Gobierno** (Government Palace) are crammed with *tiendas*, hole-in-the-wall shops selling everything from buttons to haircuts. Shoe shiners sit under the adjacent arches of the neoclassical **Palacio Arzobispal**, home to the bishop since the 16th century. Interior courtyards offer a place to eat, shop and surf the Internet. Join locals to light a candle in **La Catedral** (*Open: Mon–Sat 8am–6pm, Sun 8am–1pm. Free admission*), founded in 1535 and so the oldest in the Americas, or sit on benches under the plaza's palm trees.

You can also peek behind the partition of the indigenous chapel **Iglesia El Sagrario**, beside the cathedral, to see an impressive red and gold-leaf Baroque carved panel by Bernardo de Legarda.

Plaza Grande (official name), Venezuela, Chile & Espejo.

Escuela Taller (Workshop School)

Visit the next generation of artisans at this school that trains underprivileged youngsters. The accomplished handiwork on sale includes inlaid wooden cabinets.

Corner of Montufar N2-50 & Pereira. Tel: (02) 295 9325. Open: 8am–noon & 1–4pm. Free admission.

Iglesia de San Francisco

Quito's oldest religious complex, built in 1536, stretches two blocks and is the largest in South America. Whitewashed walls flanked by twin bell towers look impressive across the vast, empty cobblestone of Plaza San Francisco. The Quito School of Art (*see box, p26*) was born here among San Francisco's seven cloisters, three temples and seven patios. Indigenous faces look out of religious icons all over the compound, and the well-lit **Capilla de Cantuña** houses an impressive collection. It is said that Cantuña made a pact with the devil to exchange his soul on completion of building San Francisco's chapel. Cleverly, he made sure the last stone was never laid.

The capital city Quito is packed with intriguing places to visit

See, too, a fine colonial art collection in the **Museo de San Francisco**. After seeing the sights, try the guanabana ice cream sold by Micky, who's been serving it in the plaza as long as anyone can remember.

Plaza San Francisco. Museum open: Mon–Sat 9am–1pm & 2–6pm, Sun 9am–noon. Admission charge.

Museo de la Ciudad (City Museum)
Housed in Quito's first hospital, this museum brings alive the life of indigenous Indians up to the 19th century. Exhibits include a life-size cane-and-mud house spilling with foodstuffs and sound effects, a burial chamber and colourful feather hats. Check out the unusual red and gold hospital chapel next door.

García Moreno 572 & Rocafuerte. Tel: (02) 228 3882.

www.museociudadquito.gov.ec. Open: Tue–Sun 9.30am–5.30pm. Admission charge, and English-speaking guided tours available.

'La Ronda'
A pretty arch crowns this picturesque cobbled street, with tourist police a reminder that it was once dangerous. Chill within the bright blue walls of cool **Cafeto** (*Open: noon–11pm*), explore the art gallery (*Open: 9am–5pm. Free admission*) and teeny chapel and peer into the family business **Jerusalem Candles**, the last in a street once known for candle-making.

Calle Morales & Venezuela.

New Town
The New Town lacks colonial charm, but a recent refit has transformed the Mariscal District into Quito's coolest

quarter. It has all the facilities travellers need – hotels, banks, travel agencies, shops and Internet cafés – in and around its main artery, Avenida Amazonas. Plaza Foch is the hip and happening nightspot.

The **Tourist Information Centre** is next to the distinctively pink Museo Mindalae (*Reina Victoria & La Niña, Mariscal. Tel: (02) 255 1566. Open: daily 9am–5pm*).

Museo del Banco Central (Central Bank Museum)

The city's finest museum, housed in a contemporary, mirror-plated building, has an outstanding pre-Columbian collection and a good range of colonial, 19th- and 20th-century art. Among the coca-chewing figurines on the ground floor is a stunning sun-like gold mask from the coastal La Tolita people (600 BC). Upstairs are pieces by notables

of the Quito School, Bernardo de Legarda and Caspicara, contemporary works by Guayasamín, and more.
Casa de la Cultura Ecuadoriana, Avenida Patria between 6 de Diciembre & 12 de Octubre. Tel: (02) 222 3258/ 3259. www.museobibliotecabce.com. Open: Tue–Fri 9am–5pm, Sat & Sun 10am–4pm. Closed: Mon. Admission charge.

Museo Fundación Guayasamín (Guayasamín Museum)

Oswaldo Guayasamín was Ecuador's most celebrated contemporary artist. His works offer a disturbing insight into indigenous suffering. There's an excellent collection of works from pre-Columbian times and the Escuela Quiteña (Quito School) here. A ten-minute walk away, Guayasamín's **Capilla del Hombre** (Chapel of Man), dedicated to humanity, shows the light

On a clear day the Telefériqo cable car offers great views across the city

and dark sides of human nature.
*Museo Fundación Guayasamín, José
Bosmediano E15-68, Bellavista Alto.
Tel: (02) 244 6455. www.guayasamin.com
(in Spanish). Open: Mon–Fri 10am–5pm.
Capilla del Hombre, Lorenzo Chávez
EA18-143 & Mariano Calvache.
Tel: (02) 244 8492. www.
capilladelhombre.com (in Spanish).
Open: Tue–Sat 10am–5pm. Admission
charge covers museum & chapel. Taxi:
from the Mariscal district, included
in tours.*

Museo Mindalae

Built to house a museum of Ecuador's
indigenous cultures, this dark pink
museum is set over five floors around a
spiral staircase representing non-linear
time. Its imaginative exhibits explore
indigenous beliefs such as cosmovision.
Low-lit shamanic altars sport
everything from eagle feathers to
cigarettes, and Amazon artefacts
include blowguns and a shrunken head.
Unique and desirable handicrafts are
on offer in its Fairtrade shop.
*Reina Victoria y La Niña, Mariscal.
Tel: (02) 255 5394. www.sinchisacha.org.
Open: daily 9.30am–6pm. Admission
charge, and English-speaking guide
available.*

Telefériqo cable car

On a clear day, Quito's newest
attraction gives a superb view across
the city and beyond to snowcapped
peaks. A 15-minute ride lands you on
the *páramo* of Pichincha Volcano at
4,100m (13,450ft) where you'll find a
telescope, cafés, restaurants and al
fresco live music (think Bob Marley
with an Andean twist). From here, take
the well-maintained trail snaking up
the hill for even better views, or enjoy
an inexpensive horse ride. To escape
the queues, go up the Telefériqo first
thing, especially at weekends, or buy an
express ticket to jump them. Take
warm clothing.
*Free transfer ride from Terminal Ecovía,
Río Coca & 6 Diciembre & Terminal de
Trolebús, Avenida Amazonas.
Tel: (02) 225 2753.
www.teleferiqo.com (in Spanish).
Open: Mon–Thur 10am–7pm, Fri–Sun
9am–7pm. Admission charge.*

QUITO RESOURCES

The following are excellent sources of
information for the Quito area:
Quito Metropolitan Tourism Corporation
Publishes a plethora of information including
Quito maps, leaflets on themed walks,
booklets on museums, hotels and gastronomy
and guides to interesting places within reach
of the capital.
*Palacio Municipal, Plaza de la Independencia.
Tel: (02) 228 1904. www.quito.com.ec.
Open: Mon–Fri 9am–8pm, Sat 10am–8pm,
Sun 10am–4pm.*
South American Explorers (SAE)
A non-profit member organisation with a
Quito clubhouse. Trip reports written by
members are a source of honest information,
accessed online.
*Jorge Washington 311 & Leónidas Plaza,
Mariscal Sucre, Quito. Tel: (02) 225 228.
www.saexplorers.com. Open: Mon–Wed & Fri
9.30am–5pm, Thur 9.30am–6pm, Sat
9.30am–1pm.*

Walk: Quito's historic centre

This walk takes in some of the main and most lovely sites of Quito's historic heart.

The 3km (2 miles) can be done in a fast-paced half-day, but can easily stretch to a day if you include lunch, coffee, shopping and people-watching stops.

To start, take a taxi to the basilica at the top of Calle Venezuela. Facing the basilica, walk up Carchi on its left side to enter.

1 La Basílica

With imposing Gothic spires looming over the city, the basilica's dramatic façade is (literally) topped only by the stupendous 360° view of Quito from its tower.

At the top of Carchi, turn left into García Moreno, called the 'Street of the Seven Crosses' after the churches, hospitals and monasteries erected by the conquistadors. After seven blocks downhill, you'll arrive at a square.

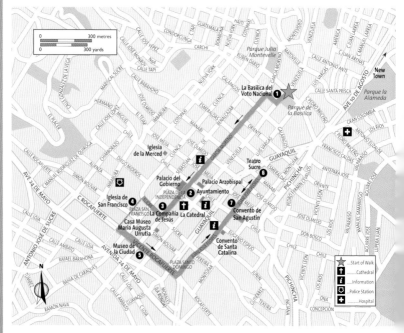

2 Plaza de la Independencia

Standing here in the seat of power in the country, and the old town's liveliest square, you'll see directly in front of you the white cathedral stretching along the south side of the square. To your right, the flag flies over Government Palace. To your left is City Hall, and behind you, the hard-to-miss neoclassical Archbishop's Palace.
Walk up onto the raised walkway in front of Government Palace. A plaque on the steps down marks the assassination of Gabriel Moreno, who took his final breath in the nearby cathedral. About 25m (27 yards) on the right is the most celebrated church in Quito.

3 La Compañía de Jesús

This is the church with the wow factor, said to be the most beautiful in the Americas. With its restoration completed in 2005, gold now gleams from its altar and its Moorish vaulted ceiling is revealed in all its glory.
Take the next right up Sucre, which after a block opens onto the vast Plaza San Francisco. Walk diagonally across and up the stone steps of the impressive building in front.

4 Iglesia de San Francisco

This religious complex is the oldest in Quito, the largest in South America and the birthplace of the Quito School of Art. Stop for coffee and fairtrade shopping at El Tianguez on the plaza.

Standing facing the square, head right, back past San Francisco to Cuenca, and after one block turn left into Rocafuerte. Two blocks on the right, in García Moreno, is the old town's main museum.

5 Museo de la Ciudad

The city museum gives an insight into the daily life and development of indigenous Indian culture in a lively presentation complete with life-size models and sound effects.
Pop into La Ronda behind it, or continue down Rocafuerte; after two blocks go through Plaza Santo Domingo on the left and into Juan José Flores. After seven blocks, walk into Plaza del Teatro on the left.

6 Teatro Sucre

Quito's cultural icon, the neoclassical Teatro Sucre's gleaming white Corinthian columns are decorated with figures representing the arts.
Retrace your steps down Juan José Flores. After three blocks, on your right in Calle Chile, is a monastery with a secret.

7 Convento de San Agustín

The Declaration of Independence was signed in 1809 in the lovely chapterhouse of this 17th-century convent. Its dome is the widest in the city, seen from Plaza de la Independencia.
Turn left down Calle Chile to El Cafeto, where you can put your feet up and relax with the best coffee in town.

Traditional crafts of the Andes

Ecuador produces some of the most interesting and diverse handicrafts or *artesania* in South America. Weaving is perhaps best known and ranges from woollen tapestries from Salasaca to the famous Panama hats produced in the Southern Highlands. Other well-known, interesting handicrafts include Naïf paintings on goatskin from Tigua, delicate filigree jewellery from Cuenca, and *tagua* ('vegetable ivory') carved into everything from birds to thimbles.

Carving

Tagua, the hard nut from a palm, was traded from the coast, and everything from thimbles to vases to animals is carved out of it. Found throughout, when the railway arrived in Riobamba, it adopted the craft. Nicknamed 'vegetable ivory', tagua used to be Ecuador's second-largest export, used for the knobs of umbrellas and chess figures in Europe before plastic was invented. It's now enjoying a revival, as the handmade buttons on Calvin Klein shirts.

Fairtrade

Buying handicrafts at the villages which specialise in producing them or from individual artists in local markets helps keep traditional arts alive. See individual entries and shopping (*pp136–41*) for details.

Painting

Tigua, the name of a village in the Central Andes, has become synonymous with Naïf art. What began as a man painting a drum in the 1970s is now a village industry, with artists producing colourful paintings on mainly goatskin hides depicting the details of everyday life – herding sheep and llamas, celebrating festivals, customs, ancient myths of the mountains… even soaring condors.

The Panama hat

The prince of straw hats and pinnacle of weaving tradition is the Panama hat, made out of fine toquilla straw from the coast, boiled, dried then patiently woven for a week or more. Not from Panama but actually from Ecuador, this lightweight, breathable, Spanish-designed hat was fashionable in Europe in the 19th century and has graced celebrity heads from Winston Churchill to Bruce Willis. Hat quality is determined by weaves per inch, varying from 100 to 2,000. Cuenca is the centre of production, although the finest weaves come from Montecristi on the coast.

Textile weaving in parts of Ecuador dates back to pre-Inca times

Weaving

Textile weaving centred around Otavalo dates back to pre-Inca times. The craft adapted as colonial influences introduced new materials to the region, with the Incas bringing llamas and alpacas, and the Spanish introducing sheep. Fine woollen textiles are still traditionally woven on back-strap looms (operated by men) and naturally dyed textiles are still produced, using substances such as the *achiote* shrub's fruit and cochineal. Everything from hand-woven belts and hair braids to delicate embroidered blouses and skirts are part of indigenous traditional dress.

Specialities

Northern Andes

Cotacachi: leather goods, from suitcases to shoes

Peguche: quality weaving, and musical instruments

San Antonio de Ibarra: some of the best woodcarving in South America, from figures to domestic objects

Tigua: colourful paintings with rural themes on animal hide

Zuleta: the village most famous for embroidery

Central Andes

Salasaca: fine woollen wall hangings with nature motifs

Southern Andes

Chordeleg: gold and silver filigree jewellery

Cuenca: ceramics (from pre-Incan vases to murals) and Panama hats

Galuseo: Ikat weaving

Sigsig: Panama hats

NORTHERN ANDES

Just a few hours' drive from Quito, the Northern Andes is another world. Stately *haciendas* offer colonial luxury amid a landscape of lakes and volcanoes, cloudforest and grassy *páramo*, but this region is an indigenous stronghold, with villages full of craftsmen, musicians and practising shamans in dizzying costume.

Otavalo

This region is centred around Otavalo, one of Ecuador's most visited sites and home to the most prosperous indigenous group, the Otavaleños, relocated by the Incas from Bolivia. Many still wear distinctive traditional black and white dress and the men sport Inca-style braided ponytails.

Otavalo has frequent festivals. For a list, local maps and information visit the **Tourist Information Office** (*Sucre & García Moreno. Tel: (06) 292 1994.*

Otavalo market

www.otavaloturismo.com. Open: Mon–Fri 8.30am–12.30pm & 2–6pm).

Otavalo market

Otavalo is best known for its vibrant market which on Saturdays becomes the largest in South America. Taking over the aptly named main square, Plaza de los Ponchos, it spills down the side streets and on its edges is a parade of piglets, llamas and sheep. Otavalo market is the place to buy inexpensive handicrafts, whether you're after alpaca jumpers, ponchos and scarves, woollen wall hangings, Tigua paintings, Panama hats or ceramics. For high-quality, hand-produced items, shop in the villages that produce the goods (*see pp36–7*), but Otavalo can't be beaten for choice.

Bargain at Otavalo market by suggesting half the asking price and gradually increasing the offer, while the stallholder decreases their price. End up halfway, with both parties happy. The best prices, but much less choice, are found on weekdays.

Plaza de los Ponchos and surrounding streets. Open: daily. Animal market open 5–9am. Bus, private car or excursion from Quito.

Northern villages
Cotacachi

Some 12km (7¹/₂ miles) north of Otavalo, this town is the leather capital of Ecuador. Shops line Calle 10 de Agosto, where a leather market is held on Sundays, selling everything from belts to

A weaving demonstration at El Gran Condor, Peguche

babies' booties. It's the only town with an indigenous mayor, Auki Tituaña.
Twenty-minute bus or taxi ride from Otavalo, usually included on excursions to Otavalo market.

Ilumán

The most famous *yachacs* (or shamans) come from this village and perform ritual *limpias* (cleansings) at their homes for a small sum. Typically, the shaman blows ginger and *aguardiente* (firewater brewed from sugar cane) over the body, then rubs candles and rolls eggs to absorb bad energy, accompanied by singing and whistling to call the ancestral spirits.
Short bus or taxi ride from Otavalo, but best arranged through tour agencies such as ATC (see p127).

Peguche

Famous for its riotous parade during the Inti Raymi festival in June, this village is also known for fine weaving, by handloom and men's back-strap loom. Ask for a demonstration at **El Gran Condor** (*Plaza Central. Tel: (06) 269 0161. www.artesaniaelgrancondor. com*). Home of the first Otavaleño band to travel overseas, the village affords the opportunity to catch panpipe-making demonstrations and performances at a band member's home/shop, **Ñanda Mañachi** (*Barrio Central. Tel: (06) 269 0076 & 099 189 262*).

Pretty **Peguche Waterfall** is reached in 15 minutes along a paved trail. A sacred spot where shamans bathe, it's a place to meet locals at weekends (*1km/²/₃ mile southeast of village centre. Open: 9am–5pm. Admission charge*).
A bus hop, a ten-minute taxi ride, or an hour's walk from Otavalo.

The Andean condor is the largest flying bird in the world and the national bird of Ecuador

Northern excursions
Laguna Cuicocha ('Guinea-pig Lake')

Sulphurous bubbles emerge around the pristine islands in this 3km-wide (nearly 2-mile) crater lake in the Imbabura Volcano. The lake is dubbed 'God Lake' by locals, and shamans hold a ceremony here during the Inti Raymi festival in June. For ecological reasons, its two islands can now only be visited by half-hourly motorboat trips from the garish building on the shore. The informative visitors' centre opens infrequently, but a simple restaurant offers lunch. For great views, trek the 8km (5 miles) around its perimeter (*see pp42–3*).

Admission charge, payable at the national park entrance. Taxi: from Cotacachi (18km/11 miles).

ANDEAN CONDOR

The national bird of Ecuador is the Andean condor, a vulture with a wingspan over 3m (10ft) and weighing 10kg (22lb), making it the largest flying bird in the world. Its preferred habitat is the steep canyons of the high Andes, where it roosts on rocky cliffsides. Endangered by hunters and food shortage, only 100–200 birds remain in the wild. A sighting is guaranteed at the rehabilitation project at **Hacienda Zuleta**, where wild birds circle down to visit those rescued from captivity. Opt for a lunch package here (*Tel: (06) 266 2032. www.zuleta.com*) or better still, a stay.

VOLCANOES AS GODS

The volcanoes were gods to indigenous people, each given a distinct personality. Cayambe, the highest glacier on the equator, is known as the shy one as it's difficult to see. Otavalo's biggest mountain, 'papa' Imbabura, is the sacred protector of the land. When Cotacachi is snowcapped in the morning, it means she has been 'visited' in the night by Imbabura, and when it rains, 'papa' is said to be peeing in the valley.

Quitsato

An independent project created by the owner of one of Ecuador's oldest *haciendas*, Hacienda Guachalá, Quitsato means 'middle of the world' in the indigenous language of coastal Indians. This modern orange tube in the middle of a cobblestone circle showing the movements of the sun is a new, accurate monument to the equator, based on pre-Inca Aboriginals' knowledge of the sundial. Information rooms are planned and a computer-generated tour looks at the creation of light effects in Quito's churches. Nearby, **Hacienda Guachalá** makes a good lunch stop (*Panamericana Norte Km45, Cayambe. Tel: (02) 236 3042 & 098 146 681. www.guachala.com*). It is little changed from the 16th century, with original courtyard and floors and some walls lined with straw; the French geodesic mission stayed and family stories involve frequent visitor ex-president García Moreno. Only about an hour's drive from Quito, Quitsato is usually a stop on organised excursions.
*Panamericana Norte Km55,
Via Cayambe.
www.quitsato.org.
Free admission.*

The Andes

Lake Cuicocha, or 'Guinea-pig Lake', is of religious significance to locals

Walk: Laguna Cuicocha

This high-altitude ridge walk around the edge of a sacred crater gives stupendous views of the lake and the north – when the mist lifts. This varied trail goes through montane forest with medicinal herbs to páramo and tropical forest.

Taking three or four hours, the 8km (5 miles) can be done by anyone of moderate fitness, after acclimatisation. Best in the morning, the weather is unpredictable (so come prepared for rain), although the walk is sheltered from the wind.

To avoid starting with a steep ascent, go clockwise around the lake from near the national park toll booth. Although it's possible to navigate alone, it's a good idea to get dropped at the booth by bus (to avoid walking a boring additional 4km/2½ miles up the road) and to arrange a knowledgeable native guide/driver from **Runa Tupari** (www.runatupari.com) who will start at the senderos ('footpath') sign on the right, taking a dirt track past a horse field for 50m (55 yards).

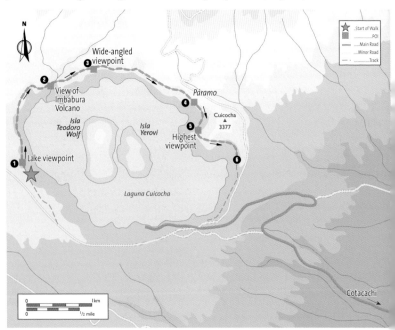

1 Lake viewpoint

Beside a sign depicting the Spectacled Bear (not found here), you'll be rewarded by the first and best view of the lake.

Continue as the path winds up the hill among pines, montane forest and a potato plantation, with the lake to the right. As it forks, take the upper path and keep a lookout for the mountain chicken. After around 15 minutes, go through a gate to the second viewpoint.

2 View of Imbabura Volcano

Look out for this on the right/east.

The path continues, although with a confusing crisscross of tracks in the páramo. *Head to the right up a hill to regain the path and after 20 minutes stop at the benches.*

3 Wide-angled viewpoint

This clearing at 3,200m (10,500ft) gives a broad view to Cayambe and Cotopaxi on a clear day, and over San Pablo Lake and Otavalo.

After a few metres, follow the 'SIGA' sign down the hill to the right, into jungle scenery, and cross the river on a wooden bridge before heading along steps made of tree trunks, with glimpses of the lake through occasional wooden fences. After 40 minutes, stop at the benches under an octagonal shelter.

4 *Páramo*

Here, at around 3,400m (11,155ft), sit and absorb the *páramo* scenery, dotted with pretty wildflowers.

Walk another 10 minutes to the next octagonal shelter.

5 Highest viewpoint

At around 3,500m (11,480ft), this spot gives one of the best views over the lake.

Climb up slightly before hitting the forest road and then bearing right on the footpath up the hill. The path soon goes steadily down through a moss-lined gulley and through forest dripping with lichen. In 20 minutes, it emerges into the open where orchids bloom year-round. For 10 minutes, the lake goes out of view and in another 10 minutes appears again on the right, with the next viewpoint.

6 Home straight

Facing the lake, the city of Ibarra lies behind you to the north and San Pablo Lake and Imbabura Volcano are straight ahead.

Continue down the pretty ridge path towards the boat building ahead and the end of the walk, where a pick-up needs to be arranged.

Walking trail beside Lake Cuicocha

NORTHWESTERN ANDES

The ethereal cloudforest of the Northwestern Andes is one of the world's most biodiverse regions, and the Quito–Mindo highway runs through some of the country's most significant sites. The area offers barren hills cradling the equator line monument, a lush, large inhabited crater and the country's most important pre-Columbian ruins centred around the worship of water. The epicentre is Mindo, bird capital of the world, surrounded by orchid, butterfly and private bird reserves, among them some successful indigenous community tourism projects (*see 'Ecotourism in Ecuador', pp82–3*).

Quito to Mindo
Bellavista Cloudforest Reserve

The bamboo restaurant of this established British-owned bird reserve in remote cloudforest is a popular lunch

Orchids at El Pahuma

stop en route to Mindo. The main draw is hummingbirds – 14 species are commonly seen on feeders outside the lodge. Day packages (pick-up 6.30am in Quito) include a two-hour guided walk through the cloudforest.

Km52, Via Quito–Mindo, 45 minutes' drive from Quito. Tel: (02) 211 6232 & 099 490 891.
www.bellavistacloudforest.com.
Admission charge.

El Pahuma

Some 350 orchid species including the endemic Dracula orchid are seen on 6km (3³/₄ miles) of trails at this private orchid reserve below Pahuma Mountain. A 15-minute lichen-clad trail leads through the cloudforest to a rock carved 2,000 years ago by the Yumbo people, and a waterfall still used by shamans for ritual bathing. The Yumbo Trail climbs to the mountain peak.

Km43, Via Calacalí Nanegalito, Nono, an hour's drive from Quito.
Tel: (02) 211 6094/6318. www.ceiba.org.
Open: 7am–5pm. Admission charge, guide obligatory, informed but Spanish-speaking only.

Mitad del Mundo
(Centre of the World)

People can't resist straddling the painted line leading through the 'centre of the world' at this concrete 1970s-style monument in a dusty valley 22km (14 miles) north of Quito. Built to honour the international geologists led by Alexander von Humboldt, whose

A hummingbird feeds at one of the lodges near Mindo

life's work was to plot the equator line that gave Ecuador its name, the architects were unfortunately 200m (655ft) out. Take the lift up, then descend through indigenous cultures by region in the Ethnographic Museum. Visit on a Sunday afternoon to catch free music and traditional indigenous dance performances. A newer, accurately sited monument can be found further south and at the Museo Inti Ñan (*see following listing*).
Parroquia San Antonio.
Tel: (02) 239 4804/6877. Open: Mon–Thur 9am–6pm, Fri–Sun 9am–7pm. Admission charge.

Museo Inti Ñan (Museum of the Path of the Sun)
This museum cuts through the real equator line and offers quirky experiments using water and eggs to show its effect. It has an interesting exhibition of indigenous everyday life.

200m (220 yards) north of Mitad del Mundo. Tel: (02) 239 5122. www.museointinan.com.ec. Open: Mon–Fri 9am–6pm, Sat & Sun 9am–7pm. Admission charge.

Tulipe
Ecuador's most developed pre-Columbian archaeological site, the six ceremonial pools are from the Yumbo civilisation (AD 800–1660) and best viewed from the terrace; one is, with imagination, jaguar-shaped. Relics are to be found in the small museum, and the Café del Museo serves snacks in an open-sided rotunda. Tulipe is included in excursions to Mindo, or contact **FONSAL** (*Tel: (02) 258 4961/4962*) to arrange a specialised archaeological day trip.
Parroquia de Nanegalito, 90 minutes' drive northwest of Quito. Tel: (02) 286 5104. Open: Wed–Sun 9am–5pm. Admission charge, Spanish-speaking guides.

Mindo

The cute, one-street village of Mindo, at 1,250m (4,100ft), is the official 'birding capital of the world'. Its cloudforests are Ecuador's most accessible and the top places to see orchids, butterflies, heliconia, bromeliads and frogs. Most non-birders visit on a day trip, but walks to waterfalls, zipline and cable-car rides, white-water tubing, cycling and horse riding are other reasons to stay at lodges and reserves (*see p160*).

Mindo has a mild climate year-round, although rain often falls in the afternoons. September–January are favourite birding months but many resident species are easier to spot in the rainy season, March–April. Avoid visiting on weekends and holidays when Mindo is packed with Quiteños. You can get there from Quito by private car (*see 'Route of the Hummingbird', pp48–9*), tour, bus or bicycle! Cycling the five hours from Quito to Mindo along the unpaved Ecoruta provides great bird-spotting opportunities and interesting changes in vegetation with lowering altitude. Book through The Biking Dutchman (*see p159*).

BIRD CITY

Within the Mindo-Nambillo protected forest and a top endemic bird area, the Chocó, with over 50 endemic species, Mindo was the first South American destination designated an 'Important Bird Area' by Birdlife International. Over 400 species were counted here in 2006, including around 20 hummingbird species. Its famous bird is the scarlet 'Cock-of-the-Rock'. Groups strut their stuff at 'leks' around town at 6am, flapping their wings and squawking like crows in a sexual display. Guided visits can be arranged from lodges such as **El Monte Sustainable Lodge** (*see p161*). Birds are most active 6–9am and 4–6pm.

El Monte Sustainable Lodge offers all the creature comforts for your jungle adventure

An exotic plant in the Bellavista Cloudforest Reserve

Mariposas de Mindo

Ecuador's best-known butterfly farm is a small, friendly place, which shows butterflies' development from egg to caterpillar to chrysalis – sometimes hatching – to 30 beautifully winged species flitting around its landscaped garden. The large owl-face butterfly flies at 6am and 6pm.
Tel: (02) 244 2712.
www.mariposasdemindo.com.
Open: Mon–Fri 9am–6.30pm, Sat & Sun 9am–10pm. Admission charge, guided tours in Spanish only.

Adventures in and around Mindo
Canopy (zipline) rides

Canopy rides offer the chance to spy toucans in the cloudforest. English is spoken at the following:
Mindo Canopy Adventure Just 2.5km (1½ miles) from Mindo, ten ziplines 80–400m (260–1,301ft) long, stretch over 1.7km (1 mile) of pastureland and some cloudforest. Professionally run and family-friendly.
Via las Cascadas, Mindo.
Tel: 085 428 758 & 094 530 624.
www.mindocanopy.com. Open: Wed–Sun 8.30am–4.30pm. Admission charge.

Tucanopy Six ziplines 100–560m (330–1,840ft) long stretch over 2km (1¼ miles), half through cloudforest. *La Venada* ('the deer') at 330m (1,080ft) is the fastest. Eco-friendly and family-run with naturalist guides. You can walk or bus there, but it's easiest by private car or taxi.
Km63.1, Via Calacalí–La Independencia, Nanegalito, 2km (1¼ miles) up dirt road, signed from main road.
Tel: 084 798 986 & 099 665 468.
Email: tucanopy@yahoo.com.mx.
Open: Wed–Sun 9am–5pm.
Admission charge.

Tarabita de Montaña

A 530m (1,740ft) yellow cable car connecting Mindo to private walking trails. It's 90 minutes to the **Santuario de las Cascadas**, seven waterfalls in primary forest, some with swimming holes. Arrange the trip through Café Mindo.
5km (3 miles) from town, no signs.
Tel: (02) 256 9312 & 099 949 5044.
Open: Thur–Sun 9am–5pm.
Admission charge.

White-water tubing

A 30-minute ride on giant inner tubes tied together, down low-level rapids on the Río Mindo. Equipment and transport provided.
Arrange through lodges or Mindo Bird Adventure. Tel: (03) 900 478 & 099 476 862. Open: Thur–Sun (or by arrangement) 9am–5pm.
Admission charge.

Drive: Route of the Hummingbird

This drive along a well-maintained road from Quito to Mindo takes in some of the most diverse scenery and sights in the country. It changes from dry, bare hills of cacti at the equator to lichen-clad cloudforest in Bellavista and verdant countryside at Tulipe.

The 120km (75-mile) drive can be done in two and a half hours one way (without stops), but it is a more relaxed one-day round trip, or even longer with a stay in Mindo. Although possible to do alone, it's more enjoyable with a guide/driver, bookable through tour operators such as **Surtrek** (www.surtrek.com).

Take the road north out of Quito, along Mariscal Sucre and then La Prensa for about 30 minutes (22km/14 miles) to the

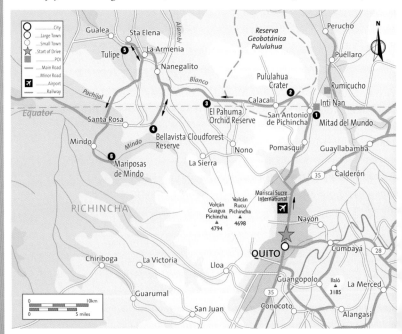

outskirts of the city, where Mitad del Mundo is signed clearly on a roundabout billboard.

1 Mitad del Mundo

This 1970s monument marking the equator is one of Ecuador's most visited sites and necessary for the obligatory picture – straddling the equator. It houses an interesting ethnographic museum.

From the roundabout take the second exit and after about 2km (1 mile) the right fork in the road. After 500m (550 yards) is a sweeping view of the crater from the rim.

2 Pululahua Crater

Take in the scenic views over patchwork agriculture in this vast crater, one of only two inhabited craters in the world and, at 34sq km (13sq miles), one of the largest in South America.

Return to the main road and continue for 32km (20 miles) until a car park and long building appears on the right and a big sign is visible on the left at the start of a trailhead.

3 El Pahuma Orchid Reserve

Enter a fairy grotto of orchids, birds and waterfalls, safe in the hands of a seasoned guide on a pretty trail into the cloudforest.

Continue for 9km (5½ miles) until Bellavista is signed just before a pizzeria on the left. Drive 12km (7½ miles) along a dirt road, taking the right fork for 15 minutes.

4 Bellavista Cloudforest Reserve

The best-known of the private reserves, this is the top place to see hummingbirds up close on feeders – and enjoy an ecological lunch at the same time (no red meat!).

Return to the main road and after 8km (5 miles), at La Armenia, take the road heading northwest towards Santa Elena and Las Tolas. After 9km (5½ miles) Tulipe is signed on the left. En route, do as the locals do and stop at Nanegalito to try fried pork with plantain and boiled white corn, the town's speciality, from one of the small restaurants on the main street.

5 Tulipe

The most developed pre-Columbian site in Ecuador, this site offers a peaceful landscaped walk taking in ceremonial sites of the Yumbo people, as well as a small museum and café.

Return to the main road and continue for 25.5km (16 miles) until a big sign signals a left turn to Mindo, 7km (4⅓ miles) away. At Mindo's town square, turn left for 3km (2 miles) along a dirt track to the Mariposas sign.

6 Mariposas de Mindo

Up to 30 species of butterfly flit about this rustic family-run butterfly farm, before being released into the cloudforest.

Opposite is El Monte (see p161), ideal if you are spending the night in the area; otherwise, return along the main road to Quito, a 98km (61-mile), two-and-a-half-hour drive.

Horse ride: Northern Andes

This ride explores the northern Andean landscape from pastoral scenery to wild páramo, *giving you the chance to experience it all like a* chagra *(Andean cowboy) – on horseback. Adventure combines with luxury, nights are spent in* haciendas, *packed lunches are accompanied by wine and leisurely starts are the order of the day.*

It's an intermediate ride with, after a gentle introduction, an average of six saddle hours and 20km (12 miles) daily, up to altitudes of 4,000m (13,100ft), over four days.

Booked through **Ride Andes** *(www.rideandes.com), it starts and ends in Quito. Ponchos are provided but bring your own riding hat.*

Day 1 Sacred legends and Otavalo Market

After a two-hour drive north to Hacienda Pinsaqui (*see p159*), once frequented by Simón Bolívar, a two- or three-hour introductory ride goes past stone-walled tiny fields where traditionally dressed indigenous people still farm with hand tools on the slopes of the sacred Imbabura Volcano. A visit to Otavalo Market, which dates back to pre-Inca times, is included on a Saturday, and in the evening live Andean music is played before a traditional à la carte dinner.

Day 2 Lake, mountains and culture

This five-hour ride takes you past tiny adobe hamlets, through woodlands and across rocky gorges and winds around patchwork agriculture on the slopes of Imbabura Volcano. There are great views of San Pablo Lake and the jagged summit of Mount Mojanda. This is followed by a visit to a family of local weavers still producing fine-quality rugs using a back-strap loom and local plant dyes, as in pre-Inca times. A stroll through the flowering gardens of 17th-century, antique-filled Hacienda Cusín (*see p159*) is followed with dining by candlelight among ancient tapestries.

Day 3 Pastoral scenes and fighting bulls

A five- or six-hour ride heads along country lanes and eucalyptus forest before rising out of the San Pablo Valley for views of the lake and Imbabura Volcano. Later that morning, crossing the plains allows riders to pick up pace before views of the pretty Zuleta Valley, verdant gorges and the *páramo*. Descending, ancient earth pyramids built by pre-Columbian peoples loom into view.

Day 4 Glacier-covered Cayambe and the centre of the world

This day is the shortest, with a long morning ride of four hours. After ascending for views of the verdant valley, the ride goes out along tree-lined trails past traditional adobe and thatch cottages, climbing high over a ridge and onto the open *páramo* at around 4,000m (13,100ft). Views can be had of the glacier-covered Cayambe volcano, as it breaks out of eucalyptus forest onto the plains. Goodbyes are said to the horses at a village square, before lunch at the old Jesuit Hacienda La Compañía, filled with roses and with its own chapel. A final visit takes in the Equator Line at Guachalá, and then it's 90km (55 miles) back to Quito, arriving at around 7pm.

Tour: Chiva Express to Cotopaxi and the Devil's Nose

This excursion offers an unusual taste of the Andes as you travel along the remaining tracks of the 20th-century historic trans-Andean railway. Part of the charm is travelling in the unique, wooden-roofed, brightly painted Chiva Express, built to resemble a traditional bus. The chance to ride on the roof of the Chiva is a highlight (ponchos provided), with the best mountain views in June–July and November.

This three-day trip covers the approximately 500km (310 miles) from Quito to Cuenca, with road travel by bus, so expect up to ten hours of travelling a day. You can also book one- to five-day Chiva Excursions through **Metropolitan**

Touring (www.chivaexpress.com), departing Mondays, Wednesdays and Fridays.

The journey begins at Sangolqui Market, on the outskirts of Quito.

1 Sangolqui Market

Pigs roast on the spit and Cotopaxi looms in the distance at this market on the town outskirts.

Board the Chiva Express at Tambillo Station, sitting on the left for the best views. Starting with a toot at 10am, it heads into scented eucalyptus forest and through villages. After around 9km (5^1/2 miles), whooping and galloping chagras race the train to Alóag.

2 Hacienda La Alegria

Traditional delicacies such as humitas, naranjilla tart and guava jam are served in the cobbled courtyard of this dairy farm, followed by poncho-clad *chagras* lassoing llamas on horseback.

Passing through páramo *and pine forest for 6.5km (4 miles), at El Boliche Station transfer by bus for the 40 minutes (25km/15^1/2 miles) to a rose plantation.*

3 Rose Plantation

Thanks to the equatorial climate here, cut flowers are a lucrative export, with many roses sent to Russia.

Continue by bus to reach Hacienda Tambo Mulao, 10 minutes (6km/ 3^3/4 miles) away, where traditional specialities such as broccoli soup with popcorn are served in view of a bullring. Then it's a 130km (81-mile), three-hour drive to Urbina.

4 Posada de Estación, Urbina

Snacks such as *chola* (a biscuit with marrow inside), corn tortillas cooked on a volcanic slab and hot *canalezo* are offered at Ecuador's highest railway station (3,620m/11,880ft).

Overnight in Hotel Abraspungo before boarding the Chiva at 7am at Riobamba Station, sitting on the right side, for the most dramatic leg of the journey. The first stop is around an hour later (50km/31 miles).

5 Guamote

Wander the fascinating narrow, cobbled streets of this indigenous village after a snack at an adults' education project. Better still, catch the Thursday market.

Continue through Alausi before zigzagging down 10km (6^1/4 miles) in 15 minutes to reach the railway's source of pride.

6 La Nariz del Diablo

The most famous and heart-stopping section is the narrow-gauge track zigzagging at a 45-degree gradient to a rock called the Devil's Nose.

At Alausi's quaint station it's back to the bus for the 110km (68 miles) to Ingapirca, a two-and-a-quarter-hour journey with a boxed lunch en route.

7 Ingapirca

This ceremonial temple perched on a hilltop is Ecuador's main Inca site.

It's around two hours' drive (100km/ 62 miles) to Cuenca from here, staying at colonial Santa Lucia or other hotels.

8 Cuenca

The final day is spent exploring churches, museums and visiting artisans in Ecuador's most beautiful city.

CENTRAL ANDES

It was the Prussian explorer Alexander von Humboldt who called this valley the 'Avenue of Volcanoes', bordered as it is by a twin chain of snowcapped peaks stretching from Quito to Riobamba. Whether you're climbing to a *refugio*, on horseback like a *chagra* or travelling by rail to the famous Devil's Nose, you'll find the Central Andes is a stunning and adventurous region. Diverse attractions range from remote indigenous villages with authentic markets beside bare canyons to the popular spa resort of Baños, dripping with waterfalls.

Avenue of Volcanoes

Ecuador is one of South America's most volcanically active countries, sitting on the horseshoe-shaped Pacific Ring of Fire, a seismic belt with shifting tectonic plates. With one of the planet's greatest densities of volcanoes – over 50 – many, still active, poke out of its parallel mountain ranges. Five out of eleven Andean provinces are named after volcanoes. Of the peaks, Cotopaxi is allegedly the world's highest active volcano, Cayambe is the highest point on the equator, the summit of Chimborazo is the furthest point from the centre of the earth, and Sangay is one of the longest continually erupting volcanoes.

When visiting, keep in mind that mountains are generally clear in the early morning and cloud over in the afternoon, although mountain weather may change in a heartbeat.

Parque Nacional Cotopaxi

A 90-minute drive from Quito, this is Ecuador's most visited mainland park. Its centrepiece is (allegedly) the world's highest active volcano, Cotopaxi, at 5,897m (19,347ft). Called 'Neck of the moon' in Kichwa, it inspired Alexander von Humboldt to wax lyrical about its almost perfectly symmetrical snow-capped cone. It's the most accessible volcano and the most popular climb

Volcanic pebbles are a common sight

THE GODS MUST BE ANGRY

The Incas saw the volcanoes as guardians and retreated there for protection as the Spaniards invaded. Cotopaxi chose that moment to erupt. The important military general, Rumiñahui ('stone eye' in Kichwa), thinking the Gods were angry at his plan to kill Spaniards, allowed himself to be captured here, giving Volcán Rumiñahui its name.

(*see p142*). Historically, Cotopaxi was the most destructive volcano; in its last major eruption, in 1879, its lahars (mudflows) reached the coast.

The Andean gull is one of 90 bird species found soaring over the *páramo* here, and birding is the attraction on the easy hour's walk around the shrinking, reedy **Laguna de Limpiopungo** (Lake Clean Place) in the shadow of Ruminahui Volcano (4,712m/15,459ft). A bit further along is a good mountain view at the Inca military ruins, **Pucará Salitre**. The 30-minute trek up to the *refugio* from the high-altitude car park gives the thrill of standing among snowy slopes at 4,800m (15,748ft).

You can get to the park by bus and camioneta or, more usually, as part of an organised excursion.

SEAT WITH A VIEW

Sit on the left on the dawn flight from Quito to Loja for magnificent views of the 'Avenue of Volcanoes' – Antisana, Cotopaxi, Tungurahua, Sangay and Chimborazo (on the right).

Open: 8am–5pm. Visitor Centre (near southern entrance) open: 8am–noon & 1–4pm. Admission charge.

Tierra del Volcán (Volcanoland)

This company specialises in soft adventure from haciendas in the Cotopaxi region, including climbing, mountain biking from Cotopaxi's car park or cross-country, horse riding and trekking (from two hours up Ruminahui volcano to the three- or four-day high-altitude 'Condor Trek'). Their Via Ferrata includes seven ziplines soaring 3km (2 miles) across a

The Andes

The snow-capped peak of Cotopaxi

The clouds are reflected in the still waters of Laguna Quilotoa

tranquil slice of cloudforest in a lava-carved canyon. The highest is 40m (130ft), the longest 400m (1,300ft) and the fastest 251km/h (155mph)! Single-day or three- to seven-day packages are available.
See p163 for contact details.

Laguna Quilotoa

Meaning 'Lake of the Teeth of the Princess' in Kichwa, this mineral-rich crater lake is an unexpected stunner in the midst of barren mountains. An other-worldly, greeny-grey oval, the lake is sacred to locals – shamans performed a ceremony for President Correa here. As it turns mercurial with the weather, morning is the best time to visit. A five-hour trek goes around the crater rim at 3,800m (12,400ft), but most people zigzag the 30 minutes down the steep, sandy trail to the bottom, although only the fit will want to make the hour-long trek back up. To return by horse, ask at the top before going down; this is a slower option, and animal-lovers may wince. Kayaks can be hired cheaply from the villagers at the bottom, if you want to paddle out onto the cool lake.

A network of buses and taxis goes here, but it's much quicker to do an excursion or opt for a 4WD.
Quilotoa. Admission charge.

FROM HUMBLE BEGINNINGS...

The former president Guillermo Rodríguez Lara (1972–6) was born in Pujili on the remote Quilotoa Loop, and President Correa spent three years working in Zumbahua.

Baños

Despite its location at the foot of erupting Tungurahua Volcano (5,023m/ 16,479ft), visitors flock to this tropical town for its hot springs. However, it's the water pouring down lush mountainsides from its 56 *cascadas* (waterfalls) that can't fail to impress.

Crammed with hotels, travel agents, eateries and tiny, narrow shops, Baños has lively charm and, at a lower altitude than many Andean towns, good weather. It's dramatically perched on a plateau at 1,820m (5,970ft), which was created by the last major eruption of Tungurahua ('Hell's Volcano' in Kichwa) in 1877. It began erupting again in 1999 and the town was evacuated but, against advice, the locals fought their way back. In 2006, it spat out enough ashes to kill animals in the highlands of Riobamba,

años lies at the foot of a volcano

MARKET DAY IN THE ANDES

Markets pre-date the Spanish conquest and have changed little in 500 years. More than just an exchange of goods in the Andes, market day is the main event of the week, where isolated villagers come to sell, shop and socialise amid a fascinating parade of colour. Try to catch one of the following:

Saturday Otavalo (*see p38*), Zumbahua, Cajabamba, Latacunga
Sunday Salasaca, Saraguro, Alausi, Pujili, Cayambe, Parque El Ejido (Quito)
Monday Ambato
Tuesday Latacunga
Wednesday Otavalo, Pujili
Thursday Saquisili, Guamote

and dangerous *lahars* (mudflows) headed towards town. Miraculously, roads were blocked but few people died.

Life here revolves around religion, partying and tourism. Baños is great for adventure, with trekking, mountain biking, horse riding, kayaking, canyoning and white-water rafting offered in picturesque surrounds. Choose local travel agencies carefully (*see p163*).

Keep your eyes open for locals making toffee from sugar cane in open-fronted shops as they lasso hooks on the wall with sticky loops of beige goo. Baños also has a row of kitchens serving takeaway, spit-roasted *cuy* (guinea pig).

Although the thrill of watching a live volcano draws tourists to Baños, there is a risk in visiting. Check the latest conditions at the authoritative *www.igepn.edu.ec* (in Spanish) or consult local papers before you go.

The Andes

Basílica

The town's most beautiful building is the basalt, Gothic-style basilica, its spires lit Dracula-style in purple and green neon at night. Dedicated to Nuestra Señora de Agua Santa (Our Lady of the Holy Water), the town's protector, the basilica has dramatic paintings depicting her miracles lining the walls, from the house saved by putting her picture on its door to a man saved as he fell from a cable car.

Ambato & 12 de Noviembre.
Open: 7am–4pm. Free admission.

Piscinas de la Virgen

The town's main hot sulphur springs are nestled below a cliff beside the Palace Hotel. They are refreshed daily, and bathing is best in the early morning before the day-trippers arrive, or in the evening when its charming pools on the lower deck are open. Although these are certainly worth a dip while you're in town, the best hot springs in Ecuador are actually found in Papallacta (*see p80*).

Avenida Martinez. Tel: (03) 740 462/493. www.baniosadn.com.ec. Open: 4.30am– 10pm. Admission charge.

The brooding basilica in Baños

Around Baños

Chiva excursions are a popular way to see the main attractions in the area around Baños. Some are detailed below (*see pp163–5 for providers' contact details*).

Ruta de las Cascadas

Cycling to the spectacular waterfalls along the Baños–Puyo dirt road was once the highlight of a visit. Now paved, carrying belching, dangerous buses and lorries, it's not the experience it was. Instead, mountain-bike on the dirt road to Patate and visit the waterfalls by quad bike or half-day excursion by Chiva. This latter does a circuit of five waterfalls, with romantic names such as Manto de la Novia (Brides Falls), seen close up from the cable car for those with the stomach for heights (or rather drops – of 100m/330ft). The highlight is the Pailón del Diablo (Devil's Cauldron), a raging waterfall 17km (10 miles) from Baños, reached by a 20-minute walking trail to a hanging bridge. Cross over to a surprisingly bohemian wooden and thatch café for a close-up view.

The Río Verde (Green River) near Pailón del Diablo may cause déjà vu. It formed part of the scenic backdrop for the kidnap drama *Proof of Life* (2000), starring Russell Crowe and Meg Ryan.

Salasaca

Relocated from Bolivia by the Incas, Salasacas wear black, supposedly in mourning for the Inca King Atahualpa,

You can admire the waterfalls from a cable car

with white woollen hats. Their distinctive, fine wall hangings sporting nature motifs hang in the town square market (best visited on Sundays). Arrange a home visit through tour companies for weaving demonstrations. You can bus or taxi here from Baños, but it's best done as part of an organised excursion.

Volcano-watching

On a clear night, the 20-minute Chiva ride up the dirt road towards Patate to the 'antennas' is a safe and popular place to view Tungurahua Volcano erupting at night. Music, campfire and hot chocolate included.

Experience the stunning panorama of the Andes as you travel by rail to the Devil's Nose

Riobamba and around
La Nariz del Diablo (The Devil's Nose)
With five volcanic peaks over 5,000m (16,400ft), Riobamba is considered the climbing capital of Ecuador and is its geographical centre. However, most people come here to ride on the roof of Ecuador's famous train to El Nariz del Diablo, a forbidding 520m-high (1,700ft) cliff reached by a steep, zigzagging, narrow-gauge railway. Opened in 1908, the railway once travelled all the way to Quito, and this small stretch, from Alausi town and back, was a triumph of engineering.

It's a heart-in-mouth ride, with near vertical drops into a deep gorge and the climb only made possible by advancing and reversing. Although characterful, the train now only carries tourists, and since a double fatality in 2007, riding on the roof is restricted. The Chiva Express (*see p52*) with rooftop seats along the same route is a better, more reliable option for the approximately three-hour journey.
Chiva Express. Tel: (02) 298 8200. www.chivaexpress.com. Departs: Mon, Wed & Fri 7am.

Reserva Faunística Chimborazo

Despite a paved road, Inca remains, and possibilities for trekking, mountain biking, horse riding and climbing the highest peak in Ecuador, Chimborazo is deserted. Chimborazo means 'ice braids' in Kichwa and this glacial volcano, at 6,310m (20,702ft), is the world's tallest, measured from the centre of the earth.

Excursions from here include an hour's self-guided walk (a guide is needed to find the unsigned off-road trailhead) to a polylepis forest on a bleak ridge, with views over Inca trails, and, for those reasonably fit and acclimatised, a 45-minute walk to the **Whymper Refugio** at 4,950m (16,240ft), the same altitude as Mont Blanc, the highest peak in Europe. It usefully serves coca tea. Chimborazo is a popular (if technical) climb (*see p142*), the graves – the most recent from 2006 – testimony to those who went without a guide.

Chimborazo is Ecuador's highest peak

On Fridays it's possible to see the *hieleros* (ice merchants) make their traditional three-hour hike to 4,800m (15,750ft) to chop ice from Chimborazo's glacier. Wrapping it in straw, they bring it down by donkey, making some into ice cream to sell in Riobamba market. Also look out for a hummingbird, the Hillstar, one of the smallest birds in the world and endemic to Chimborazo, and the shy vicuñas, a relative of the llama, protected in the wild here.

There are no buses to Chimborazo, just taxi or camioneta, but it's best to go on excursions through lodges or agencies in Riobamba (*see pp164–5*). *Admission charge.*

QUINOA

Quinoa (pronounced keen-wah) has been grown in the Andes for 6,000 years and is still used today. A sacred food prized by Inca warriors for increasing their stamina, they referred to it as 'mother of all grains'. With a high level of protein and all the amino acids, it came second only to potato and maize in pre-Columbian civilisations. Used in indigenous ceremonies, quinoa was actively suppressed by the Spanish. Although cooked like a grain, with a creamy quality and nutty taste, it is a seed. Quinoa harvested from Chimborazo is sold in shops back home.

Drive: The Quilotoa Loop

This drive is a great way to experience the remote reaches of the Andes. Travelling on winding, sometimes unpaved roads best suited to 4WD, this loop, reaching 4,000m (13,125ft) in places, passes spectacular and varied scenery – bare canyons, grassy páramo, mountains and cloudforest, and fascinating indigenous villages where women in traditional dress herd llamas, children carry firewood and native thatch houses with cacti fences still exist. You can time your visit for a market day.

The 200km (124 miles) takes two days, but you can easily extend your stay at the award-winning eco-lodge The Black Sheep Inn to explore the area by foot, horse or bike (see p161).

From Quito, take the Panamericana south for 60km (37 miles), around 90 minutes, to Lasso. After the railway tracks, turn right across from the P&S Gas Station, then left onto the road after the communications antenna towards Saquisili.

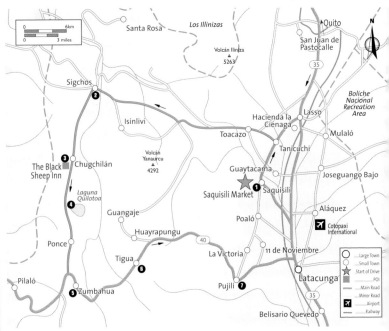

1 Saquisili market

On Thursdays, Saquisili erupts into life, as indigenous farmers sell produce in every square. Browse the handicrafts market and catch a guinea-pig sale.

Return on the same road, turn left at the Santuario de Cuicuno sign to Toacazo (about 20 minutes or 15km/9 miles). Follow the one-way system and head to Sigchos for 50km (31 miles). Asphalt paving to Sigchos began in 2007 and will improve the road.

2 Sigchos

There are fabulous views on switchbacks dropping into the Río Toachi canyon with the twin Iliniza peaks to the right. Linger at viewpoints. *Continue on rough, unpaved roads along the canyon's edge for 24km (15 miles), about an hour, to Chugchilán.*

3 Chugchilán

A small, ancient Andean village at 3,200m (10,500ft). The Black Sheep Inn is signed on the right, 0.5km (1/3 mile) below the village (book in advance). *Laguna Quilotoa is 22km (14 miles) away, an hour's drive on a rough dirt road.*

Laguna Quilotoa

The loop's highlight is this luminous crater lake at 3,800m (12,470ft), which at 250m (820ft) is the deepest in Ecuador. Trek the 30 minutes down and paddle out by kayak. *A 25-minute drive along a 14km (9-mile) paved road leads to Zumbahua.*

5 Zumbahua

The people in this scruffy, gritty village only speak Kichwa. The village comes alive at the Saturday market. What's special any day is its location – cradled within spectacular sharp mountain peaks.

From here onwards is a well-paved, winding and dramatic road, which after about 10km (6 miles) goes through Tigua.

6 Tigua

The place is famous for naive paintings, and it's worth visiting the gallery opposite this sleepy, terracotta-roofed hillside village to buy quality artwork. *The scent of wood smoke fills the air en route to Pujili, 55km (34 miles) away; Cotopaxi looms to the left, and Tungurahua erupts to the right.*

7 Pujili

This cobbled town is famous for colourful masked dancers and men who climb precarious high poles to retrieve prizes at the Corpus Christi festival in June. Monkey puzzle trees, a pumice stone church and ceramics shops selling inexpensive miniature pictures surround the main square. *After 12km (7½ miles) the road rejoins the Panamericana in Latacunga.*

Local children at Lake Quilotoa

Haciendas of the Andes

In the *hacendado* period of Spanish colonisation, land was given to the Church and noble families in return for services to the crown. These estates or *haciendas* are still found in the fertile Andes. Many date back to the 16th century and have been in one family for generations. In the land reform of 1964, indigenous workers (essentially indentured labourers) were given plots of land that carved up these massive estates. Some were abandoned as no longer profitable, but others remained working farms, large by ordinary standards.

In the last few decades, many *haciendas* have opened their doors to tourism, offering a taste of Ecuadorian rural life. They range from rustic outposts (such as Hacienda Yanahurco) to sophisticated rural mansions stuffed with lavish antiques and beautiful gardens (as in the case of Hacienda Chillo-Jijón). Each has its own atmosphere, history, traditions and attractions, but whitewashed walls, tiled roofs, arches, gardens and fountains and extensive views of the Andes are common. Many retain their colonial flavour, with traditional floor tiles, murals and colonial furnishings. Once powerhouses of economics, politics and culture, *haciendas* provide visitors with unique insight into the country. Activities typically offered include horse riding, trekking, perhaps mountain biking and excursions to sites of interest.

Staying on traditional, owner-run working farms gives an authentic experience, whether they're dairy (like Haciendas La Alegria, Zuleta and Mercedes), agricultural (such as Hacienda Manteles) or prize-bull-breeding (like Hacienda Mercedes). Some families host guests at dinner and may offer 'grandmother's' recipes (as at Haciendas Zuleta and San Agustín de Callo). Visitors may find themselves talking to descendants of

Hacienda Cusín is steeped in history

past presidents and touring homes that have been in the family for generations. *Haciendas* that are run along the lines of a hotel (such as Haciendas Cusín and La Ciénega) are less personal, but still steeped in their colonial past.

For contact details of upmarket *haciendas*, visit **Exclusive Hotels & Haciendas of Ecuador** (*www. exclusivehotelshaciendasecuador.com*). For all *hacienda* listings, visit the **Hacienda Association** (contact *info@haciendamanteles.com* or *christina@zuleta.com*).

A tale of three *haciendas*...
One that made history: Hacienda Zuleta, set around a vast courtyard that was once the scene of bullfights, is a working 16th-century *hacienda* owned by one of Ecuador's most distinguished families. The fascinating house tour reveals this former home of much-loved President Galo Plaza Lasso, who introduced land reform. His father was General Leónidas Plaza Gutiérrez, leader of the liberal revolution. Experiences here include meeting the family and riding.
See p160 for details.

The romantic one: Hacienda San Agustín de Callo offers the thrill of dining within the pillow-shaped stones of a 15th-century Inca palace – the second-most important Inca site in

An archway at Hacienda Zuleta

Ecuador – as the guest of charismatic Mignon Plaza, granddaughter of General Gutiérrez and the daughter of a legendary bullfighter. Romantic rooms are set around a cobbled courtyard complete with teeny Inca chapel, log fires, lovely frescoes and, unusually, roll-top baths.
See p162 for details.

The adventurous one: Owner-run by the seventh generation, the orange-painted **Hacienda El Porvenir** is the most luxurious of two used as a base for soft adventure around Cotopaxi National Park. As well as horse riding, it offers mountain biking, climbing and trekking adventures. It is well positioned for visits to the rodeo in January and September and has its own Via Ferrata nearby.
See p162 for details.

SOUTHERN ANDES

In the Southern Andes, volcanoes are replaced by rolling hills, glacial valleys, pastureland and *páramo*. Ingapirca, the country's most important Inca site, is found here, perched alone on a hilltop. *Páramo* and craft villages surround the lovable colonial city of Cuenca. Further down, nestled in a lush valley in the deep south, is the curious town of Vilcabamba, whose many centenarians have made it famous as 'The Valley of Longevity'.

Cuenca

Cuenca is Ecuador's most beautiful city, set along a river with terracotta-roofed houses, cobblestone streets and colonial architecture. Most people leave wistfully, wishing they'd stayed longer. Conservative, with a bohemian twist, the 'Athens of Ecuador' is the country's cultural mecca and the centre of production for the famous Panama hat (*see pp36–7*).

A UNESCO World Heritage Site, it has fossils and foundation stones that give hints of its fierce Cañari ancestry before it became the Incan city of Tomebamba, one of the empire's most glorious. The Spanish conquered in 1557 and it is now known as the city of churches, with 60 servicing its 400,000 people.

A domestic flight is the quickest way to get here, but many people arrive by road, as part of a trip through the Andes. The city is spread over three terraces, cut through by the Tomebamba River. The Centro Histórico, laid out in a grid, is easy, safe and small enough to explore on foot. Although Cuenca isn't known for nightlife, there's plenty to do by day. Pick up leaflets according to interest – churches, galleries, museums, handicrafts and nature – from the **I-Tur** office near Parque Calderón (*Sucre, Luis Cordero & Benigno Malo. Tel: (07) 282 1035*). For the best city view, especially romantic on weekend evenings, head for Mirador de Turi.

El Barranco (The Ravine)

Worn stone steps lead to a pleasant stroll along the pretty Tomebamba River, home to hummingbirds and vermilion flycatchers. Casas Colgantes (Hanging Houses) here are unique to Cuenca, the most noticeable being Casa de los Arcos (House of Arches).

A hanging house in El Barranco, Cuenca

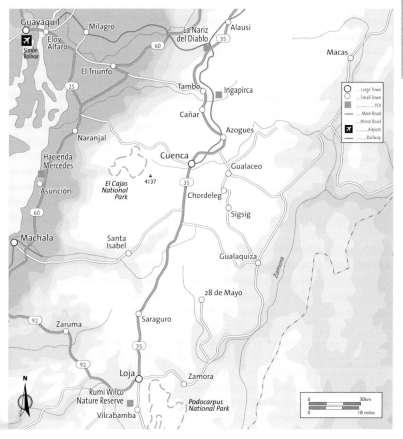

Catedral Nueva

The beautiful blue domes of the 'new' cathedral dominate Cuenca's skyline. The masses held here are the largest in Ecuador.

LA CUISINGA

It was during a bullfight in Plaza de San Sebastián that a young doctor from the French geodesic mission met his sticky end in a duel with a jealous fiancé, after falling in love with the engaged La Cuisinga.

A painted saint prays against eruptions, and indigenous sun and moon symbols are dotted around. A Carrara marble floor lies underfoot, the large nave leads to a splendidly ornate gilded altar, and light pours in through gloriously rich stained-glass windows created by Basque artist Guillermo Larrazábal.

Parque Calderón. Open: Mon–Fri 7am–4.30pm & Sat 9am–noon. Free admission.

Museo de Arte Moderno

City tours start at this whitewashed, 19th-century building in pretty Plaza de San Sebastián. It was once a rehabilitation centre for drunken clergymen, but now houses temporary exhibitions of paintings and sculptures from contemporary Ecuadorian artists.

Sucre 15-27 & Coronel Tálbot. Tel: (07) 283 1027. Open: Mon–Fri 8.30am–1pm & 3–6.30pm, Sat & Sun 9am–1pm. Free admission.

Museo del Banco Central (Central Bank Museum)

The most interesting part of this, Cuenca's main museum, has to be its ethnographic section, whose fascinating exhibits include shrunken heads from the Amazon. Tickets include a visit to the Inca site of Pumapungo outside, many of its stones pilfered for the foundations of Cuenca's buildings.

Larga & Huayna Capac. Tel: (07) 283 1255. Open: Mon–Fri 9am–6pm, Sat 9am–1pm. Admission charge.

Museo de las Culturas Aborigenes (Museum of Aboriginal Culture)

Most visitors' favourite museum, this private collection has around 5,000 archaeological artefacts, showing Ecuador's rich, pre-Inca cultural legacy, from figurines of Valdivian Venuses to shamans and coca-chewers. The inner courtyard of this colonial house has a café, with orchid garden and good handicraft shop.

Larga 5-24, between Hermano Miguel & Mariano Cueva. Tel: (07) 283 9181 & (07) 284 1540. Open: Mon–Fri 8.30am–noon & 1–6pm, Sat 8.30am–12.30pm. Admission charge.

Museo del Monasterio de las Conceptas (Convent of the Immaculate Conception Museum)

Cuenca's most exquisite works of religious art lie upstairs, among them beautiful sculptures of saints from the Sangurima school of colonial art, some with moving limbs.

Hermano Miguel 6-33. Tel: (07) 283 0625. Open: Mon–Fri 9am–5.30pm; Sat & Sun 10am–1pm. Admission charge.

Museo Religioso (Religious Museum)

Jesus dining on roast guinea pig as his last supper is an example of Cuenca's famous colonial murals in this museum in the restored 'old' cathedral. The fabric-covered wooden nave is painted to resemble marble, and the altar is decorated with a large collection of sculptures – including the 12 apostles – using the colada technique.

Presidente Córdova 6-26 & Borrero. Tel: (07) 282 5212. Open: Mon–Fri 9am–1.30pm & 3–6.30pm, Sat & Sun

TAKE A BREAK

Pop into **El Suspiro** (*Hermano Miguel 6-81 & Presidente Córdova. Tel: (07) 283 9541*) for typical Cuencan treats such as *quesadilla* (cheese buns) and *cocada* (biscuits with coconut).

9am–1.30pm. Admission charge, English-speaking guide.

Plaza de las Flores (Flower Square)

Just across from the Catedral Nueva, in the square commonly known as 'Plaza de las Flores', is Cuenca's colourful and unique flower market. Ecuador is a great place to say 'I love you', with a large bunch of red roses a bargain from a dollar upwards, depending on quality. *Plaza Carmen de la Asunción, Sucre & Padre Aguirre.*

Excursions from Cuenca to the north and west

Ingapirca

About 90 minutes' drive north of Cuenca lies Ecuador's most important Inca site. A Temple of the Sun with distinctive Incan pillow-shaped stonework sits atop a hill amidst bucolic countryside, with llamas grazing around it. It was built on a

CULTURE ALERT

Catch cultural Thursdays at 7.30pm in Plaza San Sebastián for concerts and other entertainment.

Cañari religious site in the 15th century. A 20-minute loop leads past rural scenery where Cañari women in distinctive white felt bowlers may be seen – dangling pompoms signify they're single – to the face of an Inca, carved in a rock. Many tours visit in the afternoon, but it typically rains then. Come in the morning or stay overnight for sunrise. Buses leave twice a day from Cuenca, or you can join an organised excursion. If possible, take the dirt road through San Pedro from Ingapirca to Cuenca, for an eye-catching and fascinating window into indigenous life.

Ingapirca village. Museum open: Mon–Sat 8am–5pm. Closed: Sun. Admission charge, English-speaking guides.

The Andes

Ecuador's foremost Inca ruins at Ingapirca

Parque Nacional Cajas

The *páramo* landscape in this well-organised national park resembles the Scottish highlands – a surprising sight 40 minutes' drive west of Cuenca! At 3,000–4,700m (9,840–15,420ft), its rugged rock faces and gorges are dotted with over 230 glacial lakes. Trekking is as varied and impressive as birding, with 150 species including the endemic sword-billed hummingbird, mountain toucans and turquoise jays. The most popular path is the two-hour easy trek around the pristine Laguna Toreadora, nestled in springy grass dotted with wildflowers. A three-day Inca trail trek leads to the coast.

The best time to visit is July–January. The bus from Cuenca to Guayaquil stops here, but to visit a number of sites, take an organised excursion. En route to the park, keep an eye open for guinea pigs roasting on spits, and fibre from the *agave* (sisal) plant being teased into strips to be woven into bags and shoes.

Visitor Centre open: 8am–5pm. Admission charge.

Excursions from Cuenca to the south

Buses leave to each of the following villages every 20 minutes from Cuenca, but an organised excursion will include all of them, and provide lunch as well.

Chordeleg

Chordeleg means 'burial ground' in Kichwa, and the tombs of Carchi chiefs may be buried here with their treasure, including valuable spondylus (spiny oyster shell). Visitors come in search of a different sort of treasure, namely locally made ceramics and filigree silver jewellery. Ernesto Jara has been making the latter for 60 years; visit his tiny workshop on the left of Calle Juan Bautista Cobos.

Parque Nacional Cajas is full of glacial lakes

Gualaceo

Gualaceo means 'macaw' in Kichwa, the sacred bird of the Cañaris. The village's draw is Ikat textile weaving, in the form of woollen and silk shawls and scarves still made on back-strap looms, some with natural dyes. Demonstrations can be seen in the craft museum, **Museo Artesanal** (*Loja & Sucre. Open: Wed–Sun 9am–6pm. Free admission*). Better still, visit weavers in their homes as part of an organised excursion.

Saraguro

Saraguro means 'land of corn' in Kichwa, and this village on the beautiful road between Cuenca and Loja is home to the Saraguros, relocated from Peru or Bolivia by the Incas. Their traditional black dress with distinctive wide-brimmed hats is best seen on Sunday morning.

Sigsig

Taking its name from the reeds that grace the river banks, this tiny place is a main producer of Panama hats. For a demonstration, try the women's weaving co-operative **Asociación de Mujeres Tejedoras María Auxiliadora** on the road to Gualaquiza.

Vilcabamba

This small town nestled in a lush green, peaceful valley in the 'deep south' is reputed to have the best (spring) weather in Ecuador. It's famed as the 'Valley of Longevity' and visits to venerable centenarians can be arranged

Cajas looks like the Scottish Highlands, with the added attraction of hummingbirds and toucans

through hotels. This longevity is credited to the kind climate, active farm work, mineral-rich water, organic food and plant medicine.

It was the hallucinogenic wilco ('sacred' in Kichwa) trees, used by shamans, that gave the town its name: 'sacred valley'. You can see these trees on self-guided trails across a hillside at the **Rumi Wilco Nature Reserve** (*www.rumiwilco.com. Admission charge*), ten minutes' walk from town. Alternatively, an easy trek will take you up sacred Mandango Mountain, where gold was supposedly buried by the Incas (attacks have been reported, so go with a guide), and horse-riding excursions to Podocarpus (*see pp117–18*) are also popular. *Vilcabamba is 40 minutes by taxi (try Mr Alcides. Tel: 091 921 551) or an hour by shared taxi or minivan from the bus station in Loja.*

Trek: Camino del Inca (Inca Trail to Ingapirca)

Ecuador's most popular long-distance trek follows a section of the 16th-century Inca Royal Road, a capañan *(main road) of the Incas, the 'sons of the sun', which once stretched from Cuzco to Tomebamba (Cuenca) and to Quito. It crosses from north to south along a worn stone path (that comes and goes) through wild* páramo, *past mountain lakes and ruins with sweeping views.*

The 40km (25-mile) walk takes a minimum of three days (four including travel to and from the starting and finishing points of the trek), with four to six hours of walking per day, and camping en route. It requires some acclimatisation and, with no villages or facilities most of the way, it is best done through an operator such as **Expediciones Andinas** *(www.expediciones-andinas.com). Bring warm clothing, as it can be bitterly cold, and rubber boots, as it gets muddy. For the best weather, attempt it between December and February.*

From Riobamba, it's 25km (15½ miles), around an hour, to Alausi (combines well with the Chiva Express which terminates here, see pp52–3), and a further 25km (15½ miles) by taxi or private operator along a narrow road to the camping spot in the village of Achupallas at 3,200m (10,500ft), from where you start the trek.

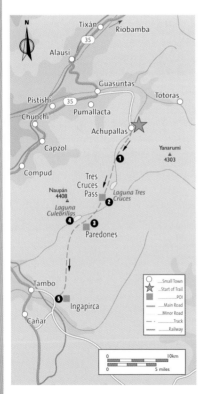

1 Inca houses

The hilly sea of grassy *páramo* of the Cadrul Valley is dotted with ruins of old Inca houses and wild flowers.

Pass under a natural rock arch and across a river before climbing to the Laguna Tres Cruces at 4,200m (13,780ft) to camp. The next morning is an easy climb of 150m (490ft).

2 Tres Cruces Pass

The highest pass of the Azuay Range is a broad sandy plateau at 4,350m (14,272ft), with spectacular views over mountains and surrounding lakes. Here, pre-Columbian travellers left offerings to spirits of the mountains at three stone monuments or *apachitas*, since replaced by Catholic crosses, which have given the area its name.

Look for the remains of an Inca bridge 600m (655 yards) from the pass, before zigzagging on a narrow trail along the marshy Culebrillas Valley to the Paredones ruins.

3 Paredones

These ancient ruins are thought to have been a fortress and lie near the ruins of an ancient Inca *tambo* (resting place) at 4,000m (13,125ft) and a quarry where the Incas mined diorite to build Ingapirca.

Walk across the path to the lake opposite, before camping here.

4 Laguna Culebrillas

This lake was sacred to both the Cañaris and the Incas and is a good place for a spot of trout fishing.

After two hours of walking, you'll come across fertile farming country at Tambo village, and the view of Ingapirca atop a hill. The road becomes 7m (23ft) wide for the final two hours to the ruins.

5 Ingapirca

This ceremonial site at 3,100m (10,170ft) in scenic countryside was built by the last of the great Inca emperors, Huayna Capac (Valiant Youth).

After touring the ruins, stay overnight at the Posada Ingapirca or continue to Cuenca, a 90-minute drive away.

Trek: Camino del Inca (Inca Trail to Ingapirca)

The jewel of the Inca Trail, Ingapirca

Birding in Ecuador

Ecuador is one of the best places on the planet for bird-watching, as no other country offers as many diverse species in such a small space. It boasts the fourth-largest number of species worldwide, being home to around a fifth (or 1,640) of the world's total – twice as many as in the whole of Europe, and with year-round viewing.

Included in the incredible range of bird species (from toucans to tanagers and from penguins to antipittas), the country has the majestic condor, the largest flying vulture on earth, and one of the smallest birds in the world,

Galápagos penguins: they can't fly, but they're still fun to watch

the Ecuadorian hillstar. A big draw for casual and hardcore birders alike is the country's spectrum of iridescent and acrobatic hummingbirds (*quindes* in Kichwa). With 130 species, a third of those on earth, these include the fiery topaz, the purple-crowned fairy, the giant hummingbird, and the Andean swordbill, with proportionally the longest beak of any bird. But perhaps the most spectacular aspect of birding in Ecuador is that, with over 100 'Important Bird Areas' (IBAs) identified by Birdlife International (*www.birdlife.org*), feathered friends may be found absolutely everywhere, even in the cities.

Although some national parks and lodges provide bird lists, a copy of *The Birds of Ecuador* by Robert Ridgely, Paul Greenfield and Frank Gill may be useful, along with a good pair of binoculars.

Surtrek (*www.surtrek.com*) offers competitively priced birding tours, and **Tropic Journeys in Nature** (*www.tropiceco.com*) provides stays in eco-lodges in birding areas.

Bird-watching havens

The planet's top two Endemic Bird Areas (EBAs) are the **Western Andean Choco** and **Tumbesian**

A young frigatebird rests in its nest on Darwin's Bay, Genovesa

regions. The Choco region includes the cloudforests around Mindo and Tanayapa Valley, where it's possible to see 300 bird species on a week-long guided trip, including many hummers. The **Jocotoco Foundation** (*www.fjocotoco.org*) protects birds in the high-altitude forest of Yanacocha nearby.

Among around 500 species recorded along the **Río Napo** in the Amazon are colourful fruit-eating toucans and macaws and curiosities such as the bright yellow oropendula, their nests dangling from trees, and the hoatzin (stinky turkey). Lodges in these bird-rich areas offer spectacular viewing. Napo Wildlife Center (and *Manatee Jungle Explorer*) offer a parrot salt-lick, Sacha Lodge has a unique 40m (131ft) viewing tower above the canopy, and Kapawi Lodge and Reserva Faunística Cuyabeno both offer unique species.

Bird-rich regions of the *páramo* are Cotopaxi National Park, where the caracara, a brightly coloured falcon, is one of the 90 species spotted, El Angel, and El Cajas and Papallacta, both condor habitats. Podocarpus National Park is one of the world's most diverse, with an incredible 800 species recorded.

On the **Pacific Coast** a diverse range of birds can be spotted in forests of eco-lodges near the Parque Nacional Machalilla and Isla de la Plata, a mini Galápagos.

The **Galápagos Islands** offer the thrill of viewing courtship displays, nesting and chicks, depending on the season. With 27 native species in the 60 found here, Genovesa Island (with red-footed boobies) and Española (for the waved albatross) are both popular (*see pp103 & 106*). But remember, it was the dull-looking finch that was inspiration for Charles Darwin's theory of evolution.

The Amazon jungle

The Amazon is the largest tropical rainforest on earth, the diversity of plants and animals in its 400 million hectares (1 billion acres) making it high on travellers' hot-lists. A vast green wilderness known locally as El Oriente (The East), the Ecuadorian Amazon is the continent's most accessible and home to uncontacted tribes and exotic wildlife. Cut through by the Río Napo and Río Pastaza, and hundreds of smaller rivers, it comprises over half of Ecuador's territory, but just 5 per cent of its population.

Day trips are possible from border towns such as Tena (*see p79*), Misahualli or pretty Puyo, but to see the Amazon proper, visit a lodge or take a river boat (*see p84*). Joint venture lodges, with community ownership their goal, offer a sustainable alternative for fragile communities fighting to preserve their forest home for the world's benefit.

The two reserves lie in the Northern Amazon, Reserva Faunística Cuyabeno above the Río Aguarico near Colombia, and the largest mainland park in Ecuador, Parque Nacional Yasuní, below the Río Napo. Lodges in these primary forest areas offer the best wildlife, whereas Southern Amazon lodges and Yachana (*see p167*) focus on authentic cultural experiences.

Staying at a jungle lodge

Comfortable lodges deep in the rainforest offer regular departures for full-board stays of two to five nights including excursions with an English-speaking naturalist and native guide. Typically, activities include day and night guided hikes (rubber boots provided) and canoe rides. Observation towers provide a view of howler and spider monkeys, toucans, tanagers and macaws in the canopy. Cultural experiences may include consulting a *yachac* (shaman), weaving demonstrations or learning how to use a blowpipe.

NORTHERN AMAZON
Parque Nacional Yasuní
(Yasuní National Park)

The Ecuadorian Amazon, commonly known as 'el Oriente', represents just 2 per cent of the whole basin but is

ADOPT THE RAINFOREST

Tropical rainforests occupy just 7 per cent of the world's surface but account for 50 per cent of the world's biodiversity. Adopt half an acre – the size of a football pitch – from **Rainforest Concern** for around US$50 (*www.rainforestconcern.org*).

home to a third (over 500) of its bird species, from toucans to colourful parrots (best seen at clay-licks, which help them digest unripe seeds and fruits). It has around 60 per cent of Ecuador's mammals, including tapirs, sloths and 12 species of monkey, and 15,000 plants, including 10 per cent of the planet's tree species (over 450 species per 1ha/2½ acres in some parts). Aquatic life includes giant otters, manatees and pink fresh-water dolphins and, at night, the

caiman (fresh-water alligator), with eyes gleaming red in the torchlight.

Listen for the hoarse whisper of a hoatzin (stinky turkey), the croak of a macaw and the unmistakeable call of the howler monkey – a cross between the wind in the trees and a gurgling drain. Household noises such as a car alarm or the error 'doink' on a computer may turn out to be insects.

All of this vast array are found at Yasuní, Ecuador's largest mainland

national park, stretching 90,000sq km (34,750sq miles) and declared a UNESCO International Biosphere

THE WONDERS OF THE RAINFOREST

Native and naturalist guides point out forest lore on nature walks: the fruit used as a 'monkey comb', the Dragon's Blood tree's antiseptic thick red sap, the 'walking palm' whose rough spines are used to grate manioc and *chonta* (Royal Palm wood used to make blowpipes). They may demonstrate weaving the leaves into neat baskets with a vine strap, designed to carry home a fish supper, or into a bracelet, later dyed with *achiote* (annatto) or 'lipstick tree', which is also used as ceremonial body paint.

Reserve. Access to lodges around the park is via aeroplane from Quito to the unexciting oil town of Coca, followed by a two- or three-hour motorised canoe ride along the Río Napo, and a final leg by paddle canoe.

Napo Wildlife Center

Situated on the blackwater Añangu Lake, home to a family of giant otters and 90 minutes by dugout canoe from Río Napo (getting here is a wildlife adventure in itself), the Napo Wildlife Center (*see p167*) is the only lodge within the national park. In 212sq km (82sq miles) of rainforest, its eco-credentials include being owned by the

View across Añangu Lake to the Napo Wildlife Center

Añangu community. It's one of the best lodges for wildlife-spotting, with two parrot clay-licks and a 36m (118ft) observation tower.
Tel: reservations office (02) 2556 348.
www.napowildlifecenter.com

Reserva Faunística Cuyabeno (Cuyabeno Nature Reserve)
This unique, seasonally flooded rainforest stretched over 6,000sq km (2,320sq miles) is best for underwater wildlife including freshwater dolphins, manatees, turtles and anacondas. Off the beaten track, it's home to unique indigenous communities including the colourful Cofán (*see p16*).

Some respected tour operators, such as Surtrek (*see p94*), operate in lodges around the reserve's main gateway Lago Agrio, a charmless oil and border town. However, following robberies and kidnappings of Westerners some years ago, the official government advises against travel to the province. Plenty of people still go, but a safer option for visiting may be by riverboat, via Coca (*see p84*).
Admission charge.

Sacha Lodge
A lot of wildlife and activities are crammed into the 20sq km (8sq miles) of private reserve at the Swiss-run Sacha Lodge (*see pp167–8*), nestled beside Pilchicocha Lake. One of the closest lodges to Coca, its unique offering is one of the world's few jungle canopy walks, 275m (900ft) long with a

The canopy walk at Sacha Lodge

43m (140ft) jungle observation tower.
Tel: reservations office (02) 256 6090.
www.sachalodge.com

Tena
The quiet, pleasant 'cinnamon capital', surrounded by jungle scenery and cut through by the Río Tena, offers Ecuador's best white-water rafting. Beginners float on the Río Jatunyacu and white-knuckle rides in Class IV rapids are found on the Río Misahualli.
Six hours' drive from Quito.

CHEERS WITH *CHICHA*
This highly esteemed drink is traditionally made of grated yucca, chewed by women to aid fermentation. It's drunk fresh as a source of energy or fermented for celebrations, but is not served to tourists.

Termas de Papallacta (Papallacta Hot Springs)

Near the Cayambe-Coca Ecological Reserve, which connects the Andes to the Amazon just 90 minutes' drive east of Quito, Papallacta has the country's best hot springs, situated in a lush mountain cloudforest setting at 3,300m (10,830ft). Nine medicinal, steamy, odourless thermal pools (ranging 36–40°C/97–104°F) and three cold pools are privately run by the Termas de Papallacta spa and resort. It has an additional six private spa pools with massage jets, lunch and optional treatments. A romantic fine mist often hangs over the pools. For blue skies, and a possible view of Cayambe Volcano, visit from December to March.

From Termas de Papallacta it is also possible to make an excursion to the

IN SEARCH OF 'EL DORADO'

In 1541, the Spanish conquistador Francisco de Orellana went searching for cinnamon and the legendary gold-filled land of 'El Dorado'. He found neither, but heading eastwards down the Napo River on a handmade wooden boat through dense forest, blocked rivers and heavy rain, enduring attacks by canoe-borne Indians and poison darts fired through blowpipes, he stumbled upon the Amazon River. The first person to travel its 6,400km (4,000 miles), he named it after the long-haired Indian warriors he'd encountered, mistaking them for women resembling the mythological Amazons.

dramatic **La Cascada de San Rafael** which, at 145m (476ft), is Ecuador's highest waterfall.

Day excursions to the hot springs from Quito leave at 9am and return at 4.30pm.
Km65, Via Quito–Baeza, Papallacta. Tel: (06) 232 0620, reservations

Let off some steam in the thermal pools at Papallacta

The Amazon River meanders its way through rainforest

(02) 256 8989. www.termaspapallacta. com. Open: hot springs 7am–10pm, spa 9am–6pm. Admission charge, but free to resort guests.

SOUTHERN AMAZON

Remote lodges below the Yasuní National Park focus on authentic cultural experiences with the Huaorani (contacted only in the last 50 years) and the warrior-like Achuar. Lodges are reached by a five-hour drive to Shell, followed by charter aircraft, or by a more expensive direct charter from Quito (visitors to Huaorani Ecolodge return via Coca).

Huaorani Ecolodge

This joint venture opened in 2007 on the Shiripuno River and offers the chance to visit the Huaorani community, which is led by Moi Enomenga, the hero of Joe Kane's book *Savages*. Guests experience the rainforest through the eyes of the Huaorani as they visit communities, try *chicha* and learn how to use a blowpipe. Adventurous trails are explored with hunters and a naturalist guide. Old women here wear balsa cork earrings, the young paint their bodies with *achiote* for important occasions and the men use blowpipes and carve canoes. A night's camping and 'toxic tour' to witness oil damage are offered on the way out.

Book through **Tropic Journeys in Nature** (*www.tropiceco.com*).

Kapawi Lodge

With the nearest town ten days' walk away, the appeal of this award-winning eco-lodge near the Peruvian border is luxury in a remote location and a chance to spend time with the Achuar, famous for head-shrinking. More than 530 bird species and 10,000 plant species are identified here – 300 tree species for every 1ha (2½ acres). *www.kapawi.com*

Ecotourism in Ecuador

Few countries pack as much ecological punch as Ecuador. Its biodiversity results from the huge range of habitats created by its geography coupled with its location on the equator. At the forefront of ecotourism, Ecuador leads community tourism development in Latin America and projects are found countrywide. Its lodges are among the most famous in the Amazon Basin, having received accolades such as the British Airways Tourism for Tomorrow award. Operators in the Galápagos Islands have also won plaudits for their eco-conscious operations.

National Protected Areas set up in the 1970s and 1980s cover around 11 per cent of the country but are large, remote, difficult to manage and, by themselves, incapable of protecting all of Ecuador's extraordinary biodiversity. National parks are often inhabited or near inhabited areas and villagers graze cattle or set up trout farms in the delicate *páramo*, for example. Old government policies often had pines and eucalyptus planted, which kills natural vegetation. Private organisations (such as the Jocotoco Foundation) and communities are crucial to conservation efforts.

As well as looking for eco-policies in organisations and hotels – from the employment of the community's workers to compost toilets – there are plenty of ways to be an ecotourist in Ecuador. Examples include asking before taking photographs of indigenous people, not giving sweets or money to begging children, and supporting fairtrade (*see pp136–41*) by buying local handicrafts or produce from locals at markets or directly from villagers. Spend time with people, enjoying a cultural exchange and learning a few phrases in Spanish and the local language. Greeting an Amazon Huaorani person with the traditional *waponi* is worth it for the smile.

Eco-lodges and community projects
Amazon: Huaorani Ecolodge, Kapawi, Napo Wildlife Center, Sani Lodge, Yachana
Andes: Black Sheep Inn, Casa Mojanda, Runa Tupari
Northwestern Andes: El Monte, Maquipucuna, Santa Lucia
Galápagos: Finch Bay Eco-hotel (Santa Cruz)
Pacific Coast: Agua Blanca, Alandaluz Ecological Tourist Center

You can help indigenous tribes such as the Huaorani by buying their handicrafts

Hotels

Amazon: Termas de Papallacta

Andes: Patio Andaluz (Quito)

Cotopaxi: Tierra del Volcán*

Galápagos: Galápagos Safari Camp (Santa Cruz)

Mindo area: Bellavista Cloud Forest Reserve, Sachatamia Lodge, Santa Lucia*

North: Hacienda Cusín*, Hacienda Zuleta*

Pacific Coast: Oro Verde in Guayaquil * In line for certification

Transport

Cruise boats, Galápagos: Ecoventura (Eric, Flamingo and Letty), Wilderness Travel (The Beagle)

Riverboats, Amazon: Manatee Jungle Explorer

Airlines: Aerogal

ECO-FRIENDLY?

'Eco-friendly' can be a catchphrase rather than a reality. Check that those companies that claim to be eco-friendly are members of respected organisations such as the co-operative **Ecuadorverde Ecological Tourism Network** (Quito. Tel: (02) 290 6021. www.ecuadorverde.com) or listed by the **Asociación Ecuatoriana de Ecoturismo (ASEC)** (Tel: (02) 255 3818. www.ecoturismo.org.ec), and book through specialist ecotourism operators such as **Tropic Journeys in Nature** (www.tropiceco.com). **Smart Voyager** (www.ccd.org.ec) is a trusted certification scheme, introduced in 2000 by **Rainforest Alliance** (www.rainforest-alliance.org), one of the world's leading conservation organisations, to certify eco-friendly tourism companies covering accommodation, attractions and transport. Choosing a certified or member company of any of these organisations means you'll be doing your bit to help protect the environment, wildlife and local communities.

Excursions: River journeys in the Amazon

A river journey cherry-picks Amazon highlights for the same price as a lodge. The Manatee Amazon Explorer *travels through the Parque Nacional Yasuní, while* Jungle Discovery, *launched in 2006, plies the pretty, tranquil waters of the Reserva Faunística Cuyabeno. Both carry 30 passengers and moor for dinner and overnights. Four-day itineraries are detailed below.*

Jungle Discovery

The pretty cedar 'flotel' takes a whole day to reach its destination. The second day is spent spotting freshwater dolphins, small mammals and parrots at a clay-lick on the Río Cuyabeno. The third day offers a motorised canoe visit to the colourful Cofán community on the Zabalo River and includes cultural activities such as preparing *casabe* (yucca bread), visiting a turtle reproduction centre and buying native, fairtrade handicrafts. Also included is a night canoe ride to spot caiman, piranha fishing, birding and native tree trails with Kichwa and Cofán naturalist guides.
Kempery Tours. www.kempery.com.
Departs: Tue for four days & three nights.

Manatee Amazon Explorer

This SmartVoyager-certified converted river barge sails the Río Napo 60km (37 miles) from Coca to Pañacocha (Piranha Lake) and back, with onboard naturalist guide. On the first afternoon there's a rainforest walk, swimming and fishing for piranha. The second day includes an excursion to a parrot clay-lick, monkey- and bird-spotting at the marshy oxbow lake, the Limoncocha Biological Reserve, and caimans lurking in the lagoon at night. On the third day guests visit an observation tower, lunch at a native house and have an optional shaman visit at Añangu.
Advantage Travel.
www.manateeamazonexplorer.com.
Departs: Fri for four days & three nights.

A Cofán elder in traditional dress

wealth of flora and fauna awaits visitors who take river trips in the Amazon

Oiled palms

Oil turns the wheels of the Ecuadorian economy and has been the buzz word in the jungle since a big discovery by Texaco in the 1970s. Hot on Texaco's heels, the multinationals moved in, cutting roads into once inaccessible, pristine stretches of rainforest and building airstrips and settlements. Lago Agrio in the north and then Coca sprang up as oil towns, and it needs no imagination to figure out the *raison d'être* of Shell, further south.

By law, ground minerals belong to the state and it's the government who grants concessions. The largest oil company is Ecuador's own,

The Huaorani Ecolodge

Petroecuador. With oil accounting for over 40 per cent of the economy, it's an important vote breaker.

With so much at stake, national park boundaries and indigenous territories have not been respected over the years. Cuyabeno Nature Reserve in the far north, where it all started, hosts oil towns and a pipeline in its territory, and its Cofán people have been some of the worst hit. Around five companies currently operate in the Yasuní National Park, having cut a 110km (68-mile) road through it. An estimated 1 billion barrels of oil lie underneath this area, threatening the future of the 3,000 Huaorani living here, already displaced to one-twentieth of their territory.

In just 30 years, whole communities have been dispossessed and relocated from their jungle homes, their water and hunting grounds contaminated by toxic waste and oil spills. The 300km (186-mile) Trans-Ecuadorian Pipeline has suffered more than 60 major ruptures since 1972, spilling 614,000 barrels of oil – more than two *Exxon Valdez* tankers' worth. Studies link oil extraction to skin rashes, miscarriages, and even cancer.

Opportunism and colonisation have seen tens of thousands of hectares of

The relentless drilling for oil leaves its mark on the environment

rainforest logged, not to mention the negative social impact, including prostitution. Since 1972, 3 billion barrels of oil have been extracted from Ecuador, yet even the small amount needed for clean-up operations has not been invested. Oil companies act without responsibility, compensating indigenous communities by creating a dependency on handouts rather than giving tools for a sustainable future.

In 1992 indigenous people were granted title to over 1 million hectares (2.5 million acres) of Amazon land, but this has made them prey to down-and-dirty tactics to secure the rights for oil exploration. It has led to the corruption of leaders and intimidation, and at least one case resulting in deaths as tribes were set against each other for commercial gain. Some Indians don't see many choices, and many end up working in

dangerous oil jobs. Indigenous opposition has become more organised, with people filing lawsuits and blocking oil companies from drilling on their land, but with just 5 per cent of Ecuador's population living in Amazon territory, without government backing, they remain lone voices in the wilderness.

A second pipeline, put through the Mindo-Nambillo cloudforest, despite protest, in 2002, increased output, promising to destroy the jungle at an ever faster rate. A massive 700,000 barrels are now pumped out daily. If oil exploration continues at the current rate, in another 30 years oil reserves will be exhausted, the last ancient Amazon cultures decimated and there won't be any wilderness left.

A 'Toxic Tour' through the oilfields is offered by **Tropic Journeys in Nature** (*www.tropiceco.com*) as part of a visit to the Huaorani Ecolodge.

Pacific Coast

Few visitors make it to Ecuador's Pacific Coast, where the 'Phoenicians of the Americas' once traded balsa from Mexico to Chile. Its Ruta del Sol (see pp94–5) passes sleepy, scruffy fishing villages slung with hammocks and housing the best Panama-hat weavers. Nearby are lucrative cocoa and banana plantations, and tropical forests sheltering howler monkeys. Ecuador's coast offers pristine beaches, and wildlife-watching opportunities and archaeological sites are to be found in the coast's only national park.

GUAYAQUIL

The first appearances of Ecuador's humid coastal capital, a sprawling concrete jungle with smoke belching from trucks on multi-lane highways, aren't flattering. Yet, although a decade ago it was a dangerous, litter-strewn city, it's now a place where tourists can stroll safely along a spotless riverside promenade to a lovingly restored historic district. More open and cosmopolitan than its northern sisters, Guayaquil is closest to the Galápagos, and a convenient, cheaper and more reliable international exit point.

Named after indigenous chieftain Guayas and his wife Quil, who sacrificed themselves rather than be captured by the Spanish, Guayaquil was 'founded' by Francisco de Orellana in 1537. The city was subsequently burned by escaping pirates in 1896.

Guayaquil's well-policed tourist district is small and can be explored on foot.

Historic district

Cobbled streets closed to traffic wind past elegant pastel houses with lacy balconies and lush gardens in **Las Peñas** (The Rocks) at the foot of the bohemian one-time slum **Cerro Santa Ana** (Santa Ana Hill), where the city started. A total of 444 (numbered) steps twist through crowded, brightly painted houses – many now restaurants, shops and bars – to a plaza with a reconstructed chapel, charmingly lit at

An artist at work in Las Peñas, Guayaquil

night, and a lighthouse offering the city's highest 360° view. Families here still eat traditional crab with beer on Saturdays. Beer is served from wooden kiosks at aptly named **Pilsener Plaza** in the port district overlooking the river. *Northern end of Malecón. Open: daily. Free admission.*

Malecón 2000

This pink-paved, riverside promenade was built in 2000. It stretches 3km (2 miles) from the lacy Crystal Palace (which once housed fish sellers and now lies near a mini Otavalo market), through botanical gardens and past museums, mosaics, water features, sculptures (such as *La Rotunda*, a representation of the meeting of South America's great liberators, cradled by marble pillars and floodlit at night) and restaurants, to end up in the historic district.
www.malecon2000.com.
Open: 8.30am–9pm. Free admission.

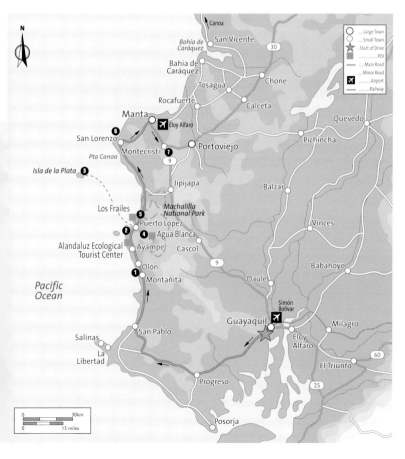

Iguanas are as much at home in Guayaquil's main square as the people

Museo Antropológico
(MAAC, Museum of Anthropology)

The museum in the basement of this cultural complex beside the historic district has a great collection of 5,000 pre-Columbian pieces, including Valdavian Venuses and a roomful of shamans.

Avenida Malecón & Loja.
Tel: (04) 230 9400. www.museomaac.com.
Open: Tue–Sat 10am–5pm, Sun 10am–4pm. Admission charge.

Parque de las Iguanas
(Iguana Park)

The land iguanas that floated downriver on water lilies from Peru now steal the scene in Guayaquil's main square. This is a small, pretty park bordered by the modern neo-Gothic cathedral and surrounded by banyan trees. Views are best at feeding time in the morning.

10 de Augusto between Chile & Chimborazo. Viewing times: 8am–4pm. Free admission.

RUTA DEL SOL AND EXCURSIONS

The road north up the coast from Guayaquil takes in a string of choice spots as well as coastal and inland excursions. The following are recommended:

Montañita

Bamboo and thatch bars, eateries and hotels cram the crowded narrow streets of this bohemian surf spot. Think oyster ceviche from street carts, beach barbecues and surfing lessons on a long, sandy beach. It offers vibrant nightlife, better hygiene and more facilities than other beach villages along the Ruta del Sol. The lovely, deserted stretch of beach of **Olón**, saved from development and seen from the chapel on the hilltop above, presents a chilled-out alternative. *Bus or two hours by private transport from Guayaquil.*

Panama hat trail

A three-day Panama hat trail from Guayaquil, with specialists **Ecua-Andino** (*www.ecua-andino.com*), looks at toquilla straw preparation in the coastal villages of Barcelona and Sinchal, then hat weaving (the most famous village for this being Pile), and ending with the finishing process in the bustling town of Montecristi. Ex-president Eloy Alfaro was born here and wore a Panama hat when in office. You can buy your own on Eloy Alfaro Street.

Machalilla National Park

Ecuador's only coastal national park spans an offshore island teeming with seabirds, one of its top beaches and the only community-run archaeological site. The entrance fee is payable at the **National Park Office** in Puerto López *Eloy Alfaro. Tel: (05) 260 4170. Open: Mon–Sat 8am–5pm).*

Agua Blanca

An important stronghold of Manteña culture (800 BC–AD 1500), around 600

THE HOLY TREE

The strong-smelling *palo santo* or 'holy' tree characteristic of coastal dry forest is used for incense in Catholic churches, to cure headaches and as an insect repellent. Essential oil and bark chips are sold at Agua Blanca.

---

stone structures have been excavated here. A two-hour trail led by descendants leads past a burial urn in the dry, cracked earth and a community meeting place sprouting *palo santo* trees to a rejuvenating dip in a sulphur pool. A jaguar-faced chieftain's chair and caiman tattoo stamp are to be found in the tiny, on-site museum. A community-run project, Agua Blanca offers a most fascinating window onto life in this spotless but fully inhabited village, with

A statue at the Museum of Anthropology

Pacific Coast

bamboo houses on stilts, animals herded on dirt roads and women washing clothes in the river. *Tel: 094 434 864. Email: casaculturalaguablanca@hotmail.com. Open: 8am–6pm. Admission charge, Spanish-speaking guides.*

Isla de la Plata (Silver Island)

If water had been found and plans to build a hotel realised, this small island wouldn't be the 'poor man's Galápagos' that it is today. A sacred spot for coastal cultures to pray to the moon and sun, it got the name 'Silver Island' from treasure allegedly buried here by Sir Francis Drake.

WHALE-WATCHING

From June to September, beautiful white-bellied, humpback whales migrate over 11,200km (7,000 miles) from the Antarctic to Ecuador to give birth to their calves and mate in a tradition recorded on early ceramics. Ecuador is one of the best places to see these large, impressive whales, known for their 'love songs' and acrobatics. Most whale-watching trips depart from Puerto López, as Isla de la Plata is a favourite spot for them, but whales feeding on nutrients close to shore can be spotted all along the coast. Bring warm clothes and a windproof jacket.

The island lies 90 minutes by covered boat away from shore. A three-hour, 5km (3-mile) eastern trail, with obligatory national park guide, leads

Blue-footed boobies on Isla de la Plata

past blue-footed and Nazca boobies (*see pp113–14*) nesting on the steps. Blue-footed boobies may honk and whistle, but they are used to humans, having first appeared on Valdivian ceramics in 800 BC. Sea lions are sometimes seen in the white-sand bays, and snorkelling can be experienced below a cliff teeming with frigate birds.

Note that up to 25 boats land on Isla de la Plata during whale-watching season (June–Sept) and in the hot months (Dec–Apr). Out of season, it is quiet and exclusive.
Day excursions from Puerto López 9am–6.30pm. Admission charge for national park.

Los Frailes

Everyone adores this secluded curve of golden sand backed by forest, the most pristine and secluded beach on this part of the coast. A path at the far end leads through dry forest to a clifftop view of seabirds diving for their catch. A popular idea is to hire a bike in Puerto López for the day and cycle to Los Frailes (13km/8 miles) and Agua Blanca (an 8km/5-mile return detour).

PRE-COLUMBIAN CULTURE

The oldest pre-Columbian societies arrived at the coast in balsa-wood rafts. Four thousand years before the Incas, the ceramics of coastal cultures – such as the craftsmanship of Chorrea and La Tolita's mythological ceramics – inspired the continent. They are now represented in museums and private collections countrywide.

3km (2-mile) walk or 15-minute drive from the park gates. Open: 9am–3pm. Admission charge for national park.

Bahía de Caráquez

Seen as 'the door to Ecuadorían nationality', Bahía is also known as an eco-city. What's more evident along the pretty Malecón is its wealth, with Ecuadorians fulfilling their dream of living by the sea. Check out the excellent and well-displayed collection of artefacts of the oldest societies in the Americas at the **Museo Arqueológico del Banco Central** (*Malecón. Tel: (05) 269 0817. Open: Tue–Sat 10am–5pm. Admission charge*) and see remnants of the Bahía culture in situ at **Chirije**, a remote, live archaeological site nearby on a wild, flat, golden-sand beach surpassing most along the southern coast. **Juliana Cedeno** (*Tel: (05) 269 2008 & 098 120 304*) speaks excellent English and arranges accommodation and excursions around Bahía.

Canoa

This bohemian town on a long strip of beach is less crowded than Montañita, with a chilled, sporty vibe and cycle rickshaws. Learn paragliding with **Greg Gillian** (*Tel: 093 972 884*) or surfing with **Mark** (*Tel: 092 877 719*) and mountain bike to secluded beaches.
One or two hours by ferry from Bahía to San Vicente (7am–8.30pm), then 20 minutes' drive north to Canoa, but a new bridge is being built at the time of writing.

Drive: Ruta del Sol (Route of the Sun)

The coastal drive from Guayaquil to Manta takes in archaeology, wildlife, beaches and traditions and moves from dry to tropical forest (see map on p89 for route).

*It's possible to drive the 300km (186 miles) yourself, covering eight hours a day for three days, but owing to the speed bumps and potholes, most people prefer to travel with a recommended agency such as **Surtrek** (www.surtrek.com), staying at eco-lodges and a boutique hotel en route. Roads can become impassable in the wet season (Dec–Apr). Ideally, start on a Sunday to catch coastal fish markets.*

Head west out of Guayaquil from 9 de Octubre, which, after 20 minutes, becomes the E40. Fill up with petrol here. Drive for 110km (68 miles), just over an hour, turning right on an unsigned main road, and after 11km (6¾ miles) turn right again at San Pablo, driving for 40km (25 miles), around 45 minutes, along the coastal road to a tourism hotspot.

1 Montañita

Seek refreshment in the wooden thatched bars and eateries of this lively bohemian surf town. A few kilometres further on, a hillside viewpoint overlooks deserted Olón beach. *Continue for 34km (21 miles), or 40 minutes, into tropical forest. Overnight in Alandaluz, the country's first eco-lodge. Next morning, drive 9km (5⅔ miles) to Puerto López.*

2 Puerto López

Catch the early-morning, beach-side fish market on Tuesdays. A good place to try ceviche, more importantly, Puerto López is the jumping-off point for whale-watching excursions (June–Sept) and trips to Isla de la Plata. Pay the national park entrance fee here

3 Isla de la Plata (Silver Island)

Walking trails lead past blue-footed and Nazca boobies and snorkelling below frigates on cliffs on this day-long excursion to a mini-Galápagos. *Excursion 9.30am–6.30pm. Overnight in Mantarraya Lodge nearby. Next morning, 5km (3 miles) or 10 minutes after Puerto López, turn right at the*

Buenavista sign and drive 4km (2¹/₂ miles), or 15 minutes, along a gravel road.

4 Agua Blanca

A two-hour guided walk with native guides leads past ceremonial sites at this unusual, community-run archaeological site in Machalilla National Park. Don't miss the mural in the scruffy little church.
Return and continue 4km (2¹/₂ miles) to a national park booth on the left. Drive through the gate and drive 3km (2 miles), about 15 minutes, along a dirt road to a stunning beach.

5 Los Frailes

This yellow, crescent-shaped secluded beach in the trees of the protected national park outshines any along this part of the coast. Walk up the track at the beach's end for a clifftop view.
Drive for 90 minutes (65km/40 miles), along the coast road, most of it only built ten years ago, to the once isolated San Lorenzo.

6 San Lorenzo

This unspoiled, traditional fishing village, under a majestic cape and nestled below a lighthouse, is the unlikely home of the coast's only boutique hotel, El Faro Escandinavo.
Overnight at El Faro Escandinavo. The next morning, drive for an hour (36km/22 miles) to Manta. Take the highway towards Guayaquil from the roundabout at the Malecón's end, and
drive for 20 minutes (16km/10 miles) to Montecristi.

7 Montecristi

The finest-weave Panama hats are produced in this bustling town, which is also the celebrated birthplace of ex-president Eloy Alfaro, who built the railway.
Return the 16km (10 miles) to Manta to fly back to Quito (driving from here takes ten hours across country and isn't recommended), or extend your stay at El Faro Escandinavo.

Finishing a Panama hat at a shop in Montecristi

Drive: Ruta del Sol (Route of the Sun)

Galápagos Islands

'It's not the strongest of the species that survives, nor the most intelligent, but the one most responsive to change.'

CHARLES DARWIN

There is nowhere on earth quite like the Galápagos Islands, the undisputed highlight of a trip to Ecuador. This volcanic archipelago, named after the giant Galápagos tortoises, is simply the 'greatest wildlife show on earth'. With no predators, the animals on the 13 visitable basalt islands are unafraid of humans and uninhibited, allowing for up-close-and-personal viewing. The Galápagos is a place to swim with playful sea lions and graceful turtles,

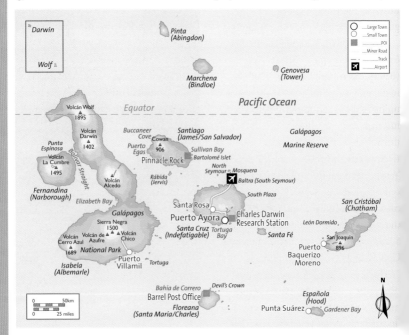

An iguana clambers over a rock on Tintoneras, off Isabela island

look a comic-looking, red- or blue-footed booby in the eye and marvel at impassive iguanas and slow-moving giant tortoises.

Rising out of the Pacific Ocean 6 million years ago, over 1,000km (620 miles) off the Ecuadorian mainland, this 'living laboratory' of unique species borne out of isolation inspired the naturalist Charles Darwin's theories of evolution. The Ecuadorian tourist board refers to the islands as 'nature at its purest' and they are certainly among the most pristine on earth. The Galápagos Marine Reserve is the second largest in the world as well as a Biosphere Reserve and an endangered UNESCO World Heritage Site.

The Spanish called the Galápagos the 'Enchanted Isles', owing not only to the mist that sometimes makes them disappear, but to their otherworldly landscape of giant cacti, basalt rocks, white- and black-sand beaches, dry forest dripping with lichen, crater lakes and lava sculpted into dramatic formations. These are islands in the making. Covering 8,000sq km (3,000sq miles), and actually formed from the tips of submarine volcanoes, the islands lie on a hotspot of volcanic activity. They range from the youngest, Fernandina (still being formed in the west), to the oldest, Española (around 5 million years old and lying to the east), colonised by plants and sculpted by erosion. Unlike other wildlife-watching locales in the world, here naturalist guides can predict exactly what can be seen where, and when. As one of the world's wonders, a trip to the Galápagos Islands doesn't come cheap, but it is guaranteed to deliver.

A baby sea lion snoozes on the island of Española

GALÁPAGOS ISLANDS HISTORY

The islands were discovered in 1535 by accident by Fray Tomás de Berlanga, the Bishop of Panama, when his ship ran off course. 'The islands that God forgot to finish', as he named them, first appeared on a world map in 1570, but it wasn't until 1664 that navigational charts were drawn up, by pirate Ambrose Cowley. He named individual islands after people, namely pirates based here in the 1500s–1700s, English noblemen or sea captains.

In the 18th century, whalers and sealers plundered the islands, almost decimating the population of fur sea lions and taking over 100,000 tortoises onto ships as live food. Annexed by Ecuador in 1832, it wasn't until 1845 that the islands were fully documented, by Charles Darwin in *The Voyage of the Beagle*. The world's last tropical islands to be inhabited, they became a national park in 1959. The Galápagos population has grown quickly in the last 20 years, to around 30,000 today, with settlements on Santa Cruz, Baltra, San Cristóbal, Isabela and Floreana.

VISITING THE ISLANDS

There are two ways to visit, by land-based tour or by sea, but the best option is a mixture of both. The archipelago has 70 visitor sites, but the most commonly visited are on islands around Santa Cruz. Day trips from here take in Bartolomé, Española, Santa Fé and South Plaza. Longer cruises (eight days) are the only ones including further-flung islands such as Genovesa. Boat schedules are set by the Galápagos National Park, which staggers arrival times and itineraries accordingly.

The uninhabited islands have no facilities, but they also have no mosquitoes. There are no poisonous creatures on any of the islands. Remember that Galápagos time is one hour behind mainland time, six hours behind GMT. And, finally, be sure to lather sun protection everywhere when going ashore, including the tops of your ears. The sun is fierce and burns even in cloud cover.

Choosing a cruise

Some 83 boats cruise the Galápagos Islands, offering four- to ten-day itineraries and carrying from 16 to around 100 people (all divide into small groups to visit the islands). Choosing one boat is mainly based on budget and desired experience. Small boats may have fewer facilities than big boats, but the higher-end choices within this category are environmentally friendly, faster and offer a pleasant, intimate experience. Importantly, they're small enough to visit far-flung islands such as Genovesa, which boats larger than 20 people aren't allowed to do, for reasons of environmental impact. A disadvantage is that the smaller the boat, the more seasickness is likely. Prepare for this eventuality so it doesn't spoil your trip.

Medium-sized boats carrying around 50 people are also a good bet, offering the facilities and friendliness and being small enough not to feel impersonal but large enough to have some privacy. Better boats all provide snorkelling equipment and wet suits. Prices for cabins generally reflect the position in

MONEY MATTERS

Importation makes everything in the Galápagos much more expensive than on the mainland. This includes guides, who require a substantial 'optional' tip. Also, remember to have US$100 cash (rumoured to be rising to US$110) to pay the Galápagos National Park fee on arrival.

the boat, with the cabins below deck being the least expensive.

Most people book from home and, for the best boats in popular seasons, book well in advance. Generally, you get what you pay for, but it's possible to find a cheaper last-minute space, sometimes on expensive boats, by turning up in Puerto Ayora. Just note that choice will be limited.

Life aboard

Life aboard tends to be pretty hectic. Typically, there are two visits a day, one usually including snorkelling. Boats moor near visitor sites reached by rubber *pangas* (motorised dinghies). Visitors are always accompanied by naturalist guides who make sure guests stay on the paths and abide by strict park rules. Landings are either dry (on rocky shores or docks) or wet (usually on beaches), and usually not acrobatic! Visits normally last around two hours and a medium level of fitness helps, although it's not required. Lectures about the islands are offered in the evening and a briefing prepares you for the next day's visits. Sailing between islands either starts in the late afternoon or happens at night.

EASTERN ISLANDS
Santa Cruz

Every boat calls at Santa Cruz, also the base for most land-based tours. The largest island housing most of the Galápagos population, it is also home to one of the most important island organisations, the Charles Darwin Research Station.

Baltra Island, across the water, is the flight arrival point for visits to Santa Cruz and departure point for most cruises (some go from San Cristóbal); the US Navy built this airport during World War II.

Puerto Ayora (Academy Bay)

The tourism epicentre and biggest town on the islands. Its pleasant main street is called, unsurprisingly, Avenida Charles Darwin. Puerto Ayora may be where cruises stop to shop (*see pp140–41*), but it's sleepy and small enough for finches to hop about, sea lions to nap atop *pangas*, and turtles to hang around despite the aqua taxis skimming the harbour. Remember that prices for general souvenirs are about three times as high in the Galápagos as on the mainland, so if stopping over in Quito or Guayaquil en route to Puerto Ayora, shop there instead.

Just 15–20 minutes' walk from the port is one of the most important sites in the archipelago, the **Charles Darwin Research Station**, the main research body in the Galápagos (*Northern end of Avenida Charles Darwin. Tel: (05) 252 6146. www.darwinfoundation.org. Open: 8am–6pm*). It is also the home to Lonesome George, the last of the giant Pinta Island tortoises rescued in the 1970s. A reminder of the ecosystem's fragility, George brought the plight of the Galápagos to the world's attention. It's hard to see George behind the

The highland scenery of Santa Cruz

The Galápagos Islands are famed for their giant tortoises

foliage, but other tortoises can be seen here at every stage of development, from hatchlings to those in a captive breeding programme put into 'training camp' for release. Land iguanas can also be seen here, along with a

DIVING IN THE GALÁPAGOS

The marine reserve of the archipelago is considered one of the planet's seven best dive spots, with hammerhead sharks the main attraction. Agents such as the English-speaking **Albatros Tours** (*Tel: (05) 252 6948 & 084 759 480. www.albatrostoursgalapagos.com*) or **Scuba Iguana** (*Tel: (05) 252 6497 & 093 008 749. www.scubaiguana.com*) on Avenida Charles Darwin offer daily dives in a wide variety of locations for beginners up to advanced, as well as PADI certification. Dive packages can also be arranged from the **Finch Bay Hotel** (*see p172*). Experienced divers have the option of joining a special dive cruise to the more remote islands of Darwin and Wolf, which count among the world's best dive sites.

museum at the Van Straelen Exhibition Center.

Bay tours bookable through **Albatros Tours** (*see box*) leave Puerto Ayora harbour at 8am and 2pm daily. The four-hour trip includes snorkelling with sea lions, sightings of blue-footed boobies, frigate birds and marine iguanas and a visit to Las Grietas, a lovely swimming hole in a rocky crevasse. You can also just walk to Las Grietas; it's 15 minutes past the saltpans from Puerto Ayora's Finch Bay Hotel. *Puerto Ayora is reached from Baltra via a ferry plus a one-hour bus trip or a 40-minute taxi ride.*

Santa Rosa Highlands

Tours typically stop at three visitor sites here. Los Gemelos (The Twins) are two sinkholes either side of the road among cloudforest, with *scalesia* (tree daisies), where vermilion flycatchers live. More

THE DILDO TREE

The commonly seen giant opuntia cactus (the Galápagos prickly pear), nicknamed the 'dildo tree' by pirates, paves the way for new life in lava fields.

interesting is a torch-lit walk through lava tunnels, which, at over 1km (⅔ mile) long, are the archipelago's largest. The highlight for most people, however, is watching giant tortoises ambling around in the wild and at the 'tortoise spa' on private farm Rancho Primicias. The lucky may even see them mating.

Bus from Puerto Ayora, or on cruise and land-based organised excursions.

Tortuga Bay (Turtle Bay)

A 2.5km (1½-mile) wooden walkway leads to this lovely curved beach. To the far right, a narrow path takes in Jardín de Opuntia, a nature reserve where it's possible to see marine iguanas, pelicans and blue-footed boobies. At Playa Manta, the next bay along, a 1km (⅔-mile) stretch of gorgeous white sand is perfect for swimming. This bay is not visited on cruises, only by those who stay in Santa Cruz.

Open: 6am–6pm. Free admission. Five-minute taxi ride from Puerto Ayora followed by 40 minutes along walkway.

Around Santa Cruz
Bartolomé Islet

You may recognise this tiny island, separated by a small channel from Santiago (see p104), from posters or brochures in tour agencies. One of the most beautiful islands, with just lava lizards and grasshoppers scurrying around its 1.4sq km (½sq mile), it's visited for its moon-like landscape.

Trail to Tortuga Bay, Puerto Ayora

The stunningly beautiful Bartolomé Islet with its volcano 'hats'

Lava formations stick up like little hats forming secondary volcanoes, and broken lava tubes can be seen on the climb up, as 369 steps along a wooden walkway lead to a stunning view over Sullivan Bay on the other side. The two white sandy coves, separated by a ridge in the middle, are made of volcanic formations such as lava tubes and spatter cones. Snorkelling around the dramatic Pinnacle Rock, an eroded tuff cone, from a golden sand beach is a highlight, with the chance to see penguins and white-tipped sharks. This is also the best place to swim with sea lions.

Included on land-based day trips and cruise itineraries.

Española (Hood)

The oldest island in the archipelago, a walk along a 2km (1⅓-mile) rocky trail from **Punta Suárez** leads through one of the most impressive and varied colonies of seabirds in the Galápagos as well as past a blowhole. Unique creatures include the green and red 'Christmas' iguana, and the waved albatross endemic to this island is the big draw, breeding from March to December, when it flies back to Peru. **Gardener Bay** on the northeast is a place to swim near sea lions who snooze oblivious on the powder-white beach. *Visited on day trips from Santa Cruz and most cruise itineraries.*

Mosquera

This small strip of sand surrounded by basalt rocks in between North Seymour and Baltra has one of the archipelago's largest colonies of sea lions. *A short hop from Santa Cruz, often visited on the first day of cruise itineraries.*

Plaza Sur (South Plaza)

A trail surrounded by a large colony of sea lions and land iguanas heads up this 1.5km-long (1-mile) tilted cliff of lava for views of the red-billed tropic bird and swallow-tailed gull. Succulent sesuvium, turning red in season, covers the island like a carpet.
Visited on day trips from Santa Cruz.

Rábida (Jervis)

With the most diverse volcanic landscape of the islands – including a red-sand beach populated by sea lions – Rábida is considered the geographic heart of the archipelago. Great flamingos can be seen in a salt-water lagoon and brown pelicans nest in the mangrove on its far side. Some of the archipelago's best snorkelling can be found here.
Visited on day trips from Santa Cruz.

Santa Fé

The stunning, white-sand cove here is one of the archipelago's prettiest spots and a good place to see land iguanas. An easy trail leads through a giant opuntia cactus garden, and a steep trail leads to a great island view. Good snorkelling here includes a chance to see the white-tipped reef shark.
Visited on day trips from Santa Cruz.

Santiago

This dramatic island is covered with lava flows and arid vegetation. A 2km (1¼-mile) hike along the shoreline from Puerto Egas (James Bay) on the west coast leads past oystercatchers and Sally Lightfoot crabs to a favoured spot of the Galápagos fur seal. Buccaneer Cove to the north was a favourite refuge for pirate ships from the 1500s to the 1700s.

Sea lions rest on the beach, Mosquera

Sally Lightfoot crabs squaring up for a fight

Included on day trips from Santa Cruz and cruise itineraries.

Seymour Norte (North Seymour)

This flat, arid island is the place to see frigate birds nesting in ghostly *palo santo* trees. The trail also loops past a colony of blue-footed boobies.
Visited on day trips from Santa Cruz.

Outer eastern islands

Floreana (Santa María/Charles)

This was the first island of the Galápagos to be inhabited. Only around 100 people now live on this little-visited, once very fashionable island, which was the scene of a scandalous mystery involving an Austrian baroness (who moved here with her two lovers) and people disappearing or ending up dead. This island is now best known for its flamingos, but they have not nested here lately, so it features less on itineraries. Punta Cormorán offers excellent swimming and the Devil's Crown, an offshore collapsed caldera, great snorkelling, but most itineraries head to **Bahía de Correro** (Post Office Bay). Whalers set up the post office barrel, which led to the tradition of visitors taking home mail to their country from the barrel, and joining the mail trail by leaving their own card or letter for someone else to carry home.
Visited on some cruise itineraries.

Genovesa (Tower)

It's easy to see how the far-flung, horseshoe-shaped Genovesa Island represents the arms of a sunken crater. **Prince Philip's Steps**, steep rocky steps cut for Prince Philip's visit in 1964, lead 90m (300ft) up the crater face to a plateau covered with seabirds, making it a favourite with birders. Some 140,000 Nazca boobies live here, but the island's most famous draw is the striking red-footed booby with turquoise beak that nests in the *palo santo* trees. In breeding season, storm petrels circle frenetically above their nests built in cracks of rock on the shoreline. A *panga* ride leads to nocturnal fur seals that hang out on the rocks beside the water near a deep-water snorkelling spot. At the pretty, white-sand **Darwin Bay**, in the curve of the crater's arms, great frigate birds are seen nesting among the saltbush along with more red-footed boobies.
Visited on longer small-boat cruise itineraries only.

San Cristóbal (Chatham)

Once ruled by despot Manuel J Cobos, assassinated by his workers in 1904, this older island is suited to agriculture and about 5,000 people now live here. The sleepy fishing village, Puerto Baquerizo Moreno, is the provincial capital of the Galápagos. Island attractions include **El Junco**, the only freshwater lagoon in the archipelago, a good place for birding, and just a pleasant bike ride away from the capital, although it's closed at the time of writing due to a dilemma regarding what to do about the tilapia someone introduced. Some

A pair of courting Nazca boobies on Prince Philip's Steps, Genovesa

Kayaking on San Cristóbal

of the world's best surfing (for the experienced) is found at **Punta Carola** near the small **Museum of Human History**. Most cruise itineraries offer a whistle-stop tour through the nature and settlement of the islands. Dolphins can sometimes be seen during a circumnavigation of **León Dormido** (Sleeping Lion), a tuff cone (nicknamed Kicker Rock) with a channel eroded through it off the coast.

Visited on most cruise itineraries, but you can also get direct flights from Quito or Guayaquil, the starting point for some cruises. Alternatively, boats go from Puerto Ayora on Tuesdays and Fridays.

CHARLES DARWIN

Englishman Charles Darwin attempted to study medicine and to qualify for the clergy, before finding his passion in natural history and geology. In 1835, the 26-year-old naturalist cruised the Galápagos Islands for five weeks aboard the HMS *Beagle*, visiting San Cristóbal, Floreana, Isabela and Santiago. Observing this 'living laboratory of evolution', he noticed that species from the same ancestor had adapted differently in isolation. The rather unremarkable bird, now known as Darwin's finch, sparked a process that led to the controversial ideas questioning man's divine origin in *The Origin of Species* a quarter of a century later. Charles Darwin died in 1882, having caused a scientific revolution, and is one of the most important figures of universal thought.

WESTERN ISLANDS
Fernandina (Narborough)

Beyond the mangrove fringe of this, the archipelago's youngest and most pristine island, where penguins can be glimpsed, is the world's largest colony of marine iguanas sunning themselves on basalt rocks. Picturesque lava fields are seen at the main visitor site, **Punta Espinosa** (Spiny Point), whose star sight is the flightless cormorant, which still spreads its unnecessary wings to dry in the sun.

Visited on longer cruise itineraries.

Christmas iguana, Fernandina

Isabela (Albemarle)

This large, sprawling island of cracked lava formed from six fused volcanoes occupies over half the archipelago's territory. Discovered by General Albemarle, it was settled around 100 years ago by entrepreneur Antonio Gil, and most of the 2,500 islanders are his descendants.

Darwin once visited the now graffiti- and guano-splattered **Tagus Cove** landing site where a trail up a steep wooden walkway leads to **Darwin's Lake**, a beautiful aquamarine pool glimpsed through ghostly *palo santo* trees, and a tuff cone overlooking Isabela's eerie volcanic landscape. A *panga* ride along the cliff offers a glimpse of 'jackass' penguins, sea lions, pelicans and blue-footed boobies. A jaunt further south to **Elizabeth Bay** offers a chance to see turtles, white-tipped reef sharks and rays.

Selective sites are included on the itineraries of faster boats.

Puerto Villamil and around

With a rocky, difficult harbour, Isabela's only town isn't on cruise itineraries and so is a refreshingly different land base. It's set on a pristine 3km (2-mile) beach, with diving pelicans, scuttling ghost crabs and oystercatchers running in the shallows. Nearby are the archipelago's largest wetlands (*see pp110–11*). A single, paved road leads to the highlands beyond the sandy main street, Antonio Gil.

A 15-minute drive out of town (or 1.2km/³⁄₄ mile on a wooden walkway a short way along the beach road) is the **Giant Tortoise Breeding Centre** (*run by the Parque Nacional de Galápagos. Avenida Antonio Gil, Puerto Villamil, Isabela. Tel: (05) 252 9178. Admission charge*). Flat shell tortoises are the most unusual of five species living around Isabela's volcanoes, and around 70 were airlifted from Cerro Azul's 1998 eruption. The introduction of their babies into the wild is explained in the interactive visitor's centre here.

Sierra Negra is another sight worth seeing (*Admission charge*). This 10km-wide (6-mile) crater, half-filled with lava from its 2005 eruption, is the world's second-largest. Excursions typically head along the rim by horseback, and a one-hour guided walk then takes you through lava fields to desolate **Volcán Chico** and sulphurous fumeroles. On the other side is **Volcán de Azufre**.

Boat excursions from Puerto Villamil are also possible (contact **Tropic Journeys in Nature**, *www.tropiceco. com*). Five minutes from the dock is mangrove-fringed rocky **Tintoreras Island**, named after the white-tipped reef shark seen swimming in a lava channel beside the path. Isabela's marine iguanas are also seen here, the largest on the Galápagos, and if you go snorkelling here you may well find yourself among turtles. An hour's boat ride from the dock at Puerto Villamil leads to arches and tunnels created by submerged lava tubes known as **Los Túneles**, where snorkelling will bring you near manta rays, turtles and sea lions. **Tortuga Island** (Tortoise Island) is included on excursions from Isabela and Santa Cruz, and is one of the Galápagos' main seabird nesting sites. Here you'll see the great frigate, blue-footed booby, swallow-tailed gull and red-billed tropic bird.

Access is by flight via Baltra, or by speedboat (two or three hours) from Puerto Ayora.

ding along the rim of Sierra Negra

Cycle ride: Southern Isabela

Southern Isabela is home to the archipelago's largest wetlands, and a grim reminder of a penal past.

This diverse 8km (5-mile) ride (each way), includes around 3km (2 miles) of walking to well-marked points of natural interest and is suitable for the averagely fit.

For bicycle hire, go to Bazar Veronica opposite the National Parks Office (see p173).

The minimum four-hour round trip can be done alone, but a guide brings it alive. Ecotourism operator **Tropic Journeys in Nature** (*www.tropiceco. com*) include it in their 'Galápagos: the path less travelled' tour.

Pick up a free copy of the booklet Walking through the Wetlands of Isabela *from the National Parks Office to help you interpret the numbered stakes along the way.*

Head away from the port along Antonio

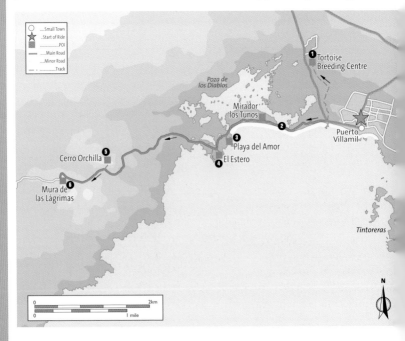

Gil for about five minutes, until the road becomes sandy and the beach appears on the left. About 200m (220 yards) on the right is a sign at the start of a raised wooden walkway.

1 Tortoise Breeding Centre

Leave bicycles unlocked by the road and walk for 1.2km (³/4 mile) past mangrove-fringed lagoons, lava fields and dry forest to learn about the plight of the Isabela tortoise.
Walk back to the road and continue riding for another 1km (²/3 mile), until you see the next stop signed on the right-hand side.

2 Poza de los Diablos

Galápagos' largest coastal lagoon is the main nesting site for the endangered Galápagos flamingo, seen here between January and May.
Ride now on gravel through a tunnel of poison apple trees, stopping at Mirador os Tunos for a glimpse of a thousand-year-old candelabra cactus forest surrounding a green lagoon. After 2.5km (1¹/2 miles) the next stop is signed left at a small roundabout.

3 Playa del Amor

This lovers' beach, tucked away from the road, lies next to a marine iguana nesting site. Outside of nesting season, a circular 300m (330-yard) walk leads past their cracked lava tube domes and to a peek inside a large pipe-like lava tube extending into the sea.

Continue along the road for another 300m (330 yards), looking for a sign on the left.

4 El Estero

A pretty track past the largest black mangrove trees on the islands leads through a mangrove tunnel to a beachside freshwater spring (at low tide). On the return, a path to the left leads to rocks, then left again to a blue-footed booby colony.
A hilly ride through giant opuntia cacti and palo santo forest for 2km (1¹/4 miles) leads to a wooden walkway up to a viewpoint on the right.

5 Cerro Orchilla

Climb up for an incredible 360° view over the wetlands, with curious mockingbirds hopping nearby. Puerto Villamil lies in front, to the right is Tortuga Island, and behind, Sierra Negra looms out of the mist.
Riding over the small hills to the Mura de las Lágrimas makes you appreciate the last stop's name (Wall of Tears). Prisoners were forced to carry enormous lava rocks along this route.

6 Mura de las Lágrimas

This 9m-high (30ft) wall is a sad reminder of the notorious penal colony that was here in the 1950s. Of the 400 prisoners forced to build it, only half survived.
The 8km (5 miles) back to Puerto Villamil is a fast and easy, mainly downhill, ride.

Nature and conservation in the Galápagos

The remote and fantastical Galápagos Islands are famous for their abundant wildlife, much of it endemic and fearless due to the lack of natural predators. The giant tortoise that gave the island its name arrived, like all the wildlife, accidentally, on floating vegetation carried by sea currents. Wind and ocean currents, as well as the islands' age and habitation, determine climate and distribution and abundance of species. Strange sights are guaranteed, whether cold-water sea lions lazing under tropical mangrove or tropical seabirds sitting paces away from penguins. The lunar landscape throughout has every formation, from tuff cones to lava tubes made of a'a (what the Hawaiians cried when they walked barefoot on this type of quick-drying, ragged lava) or smoother pahoehoe lava, both of which are like hardened mousse and sprout everything from lichen and opuntia cactus to saltbush and ghostly palo santo (holy tree). Most islands are arid, although the larger ones have lush highlands.

Nowhere in the world is the evolution of species demonstrated so clearly as here, where isolation led both to the development and protection of unique species. The dull-looking finch, responsible for Darwin's revolutionary theory, evolved into 13 varieties, from a 'vampire' to a big-beaked cactus finch and a tool-holding woodpecker finch.

Wildlife-watching

Some wildlife is commonly seen on a trip to the Galápagos, whereas other species are only found on a certain part of one island.

A turtle and sea lion, Fernandina

Sally Lightfoot crabs can be quite nervous

lazing blissfully on the beaches are commonly seen. The skittish **Sally Lightfoot crab**, with its bright orange shell and turquoise underbelly, is often nearby.

Spitting, hissing, charcoal-coloured **marine iguanas**, the planet's only bathing lizard, are usually found in a pile drying off, blending with the basalt. The large, macho, red and green **Christmas iguana** is particularly spectacular on Española in mating season (Jan–Mar).

Bird-watching

Of the 19 seabird species that breed in the Galápagos, seven are endemic. T-shirts announce 'I Love Boobies' in town, and the comic-looking **blue-footed booby** is certainly a favourite. 'Booby' is derived from the Spanish word *bobo*, meaning 'clown'. It has a spectacular courtship display in which the males 'dance', showing off their turquoise feet, opening their wings wide and sky-pointing with their beaks (Nov–Dec). Males whistle and females honk, making it easy to tell

The diversity of marine life that can be seen while snorkelling ranges from **parrotfish** to **rays** to **white-tipped reef sharks**. And there are chances to swim with **green turtles** or playful **sea lion pups**, and to spot **whales** and **dolphins** on cruise crossings.

On land, the archaic **giant tortoises** found in the archipelago's highlands and volcanoes represent the earth's largest wild population. They are one of the world's most hardy creatures, and 11 species live here, from domed to saddle to flat-backed. An adult tortoise may take six hours to walk 1km (½ mile), but it can last a year without food and water.

With 16,000 **sea lions** here, colonies of a bull and his harem

ANIMAL ENTERTAINMENT

May to December is the breeding season for marine creatures, when up-welling brings nutrient-rich waters for feeding their young. December to April is the season of plenty on land, with lush foliage due to rain, and is the breeding time for land animals. In any month, seabirds will be courting, nesting or feeding chicks.

LEAVE ONLY FOOTPRINTS

* Don't disturb or remove plants, rocks or animals
* Don't take any live material (including sand) to islands
* Don't take food and drink (except water) to uninhabited islands
* Don't touch, startle or feed animals, keep your distance and avoid using your camera flash
* Don't leave rubbish on islands or throw it overboard
* Don't stray from marked trails, stay with your naturalist guide at all times
* Don't buy souvenirs made of native products (except wood)
* Don't smoke on the islands

From the Galápagos National Park Service

them apart. The white and black endemic **Nazca (masked) booby**, recognised by its Simpsons-style hairdo, has the rather alarming practice of encouraging the fittest chick to eat the other if two arrive.

The world's largest population of the attractive **red-footed booby** is found only on Genovesa. You can support seabird conservation by adopting a booby at **Galápagos Trust Conservation** (*www.savegalapagos.org*).

Both the **great** and the **magnificent** (slightly bigger) male **frigate birds**, named after pirates because they steal other birds' food, have one of the most spectacular courtship behaviours, puffing up a bright red sac underneath their chin, spreading and swivelling huge wings and calling out to over-flying females. The **waved albatross** endemic to Española is also a favourite attraction and, with a minimum wingspan of 2m (7ft), their flight is a thrill to behold – their muppet-faced chicks even more so.

A hawk eyes up a pair of iguanas, Española

Endemic gulls include the plain but endangered **lava gull** and the prettier, and ubiquitous, nocturnal **swallow-tailed gull**, with red feet and a red-ringed eye. Another pretty seabird seen soaring up cliff-faces is the beautiful **red-billed tropic bird**. Interesting from an evolutionary point of view is the endemic **flightless cormorant**, which still holds its stunted wings out to dry, and the **Galápagos penguin**, the only penguin living north of the equator.

Among the 22 endemic landbirds, thought to have arrived from South America, there is a good chance of seeing the fearless **Galápagos hawk**, **Galápagos dove** and different **mockingbirds**, which feed on the opuntia cactus.

Conservation of the islands

Declared a UNESCO World Heritage Site in danger, the Galápagos Islands have been suffering ever since humans arrived. Unwanted animals such as rats, mice, geckos, ants, wasps and frogs arrived accidentally on cargo ships, and early settlers introduced pests such as devil's grass, guava, cats, goats, donkeys and pigs. These compete for space and resources and feed on native plants and animals; goats strip vegetation, leaving nothing for tortoises to eat, for example. A captive breeding programme and radical eradication

Red-footed booby, Genovesa

programme, quotas to limit over-fishing and attempted removal of illegal immigrants have all been implemented. In 2007, the Charles Darwin Research Station announced that the Galápagos were in the best state of conservation for 100 years. As isolation is its best protection, humans remain the islands' greatest challenge.

Neglecting waste management issues leads to turtles eating plastic bags, thinking they're jellyfish, and sea lions getting tangled in discarded fishing nets. Tourists can assist with coast clearing once a month, visiting places others don't go, with **Fundación Galápagos** (*Tel: 099 706 8680. www.fundaciongalapagos.org*), set up by Metropolitan Touring.

Getting away from it all

It would be easy to argue that, aside from a few tourist magnets, all of mainland Ecuador is off the beaten track. Attractions themselves are often about being in nature, from birding in Mindo to visiting volcanoes to flying across acres of Amazon jungle to a lodge. To get off the tourist trail is easy – by visiting lesser-known national parks without a soul in sight, by joining fabulous community projects from the Andes to the Amazon, or by stepping back centuries in a gem of a gold-mining town hidden by barren mountains.

NATIONAL PARKS

Despite their status as designated World Heritage Sites, geobotanic reserves, Important Bird Areas and so on, outside of Cotopaxi, the Galápagos, Yasuní and El Cajas, Ecuador's national parks are little visited. Those detailed below are accessible, biodiverse and often completely undisturbed.

Northern Andes
Reserva Ecológica El Ángel

Condors once swooped down on unsuspecting rodents here on this protected, high-altitude páramo, special because of its unique frailejones, 2m-high (6½ft) delicate shrubs with hairy leaves. Some of the highest-growing trees, above 4,000m (13,125ft), are the polylepis (paperbark) trees, seen in the reserve here, with their twisted trunks and flaky reddish-brown peeling bark. You can stay on the reserve, a four-hour drive north of Quito, at the Polylepis Lodge (*see p159*) for a night walk through the fairy-like polylepis forest, with myths and legends provided by a native guide. Catch a bus from Quito then a taxi from El Ángel town, or book an excursion through Metropolitan Touring (*see p127*).
Admission charge.

Central Andes
Hacienda Manteles

In a remote valley 20km (12 miles) from Baños, this is a gateway to a private, orchid-filled cloudforest in the little-known Parque Nacional Llanganates, said to be the burial place of the lost gold of the Inca emperor Atahualpa. The *hacienda* also offers trips to Ecuador's largest Parque Nacional Sangay nearby, with over 300 lagoons in the *páramo* and the most active volcano in Ecuador. The *hacienda* itself is a safe spot to sit in an outdoor Jacuzzi® and view Tungurahua erupting at night, and to see the spectacled bear in blueberry season. Hiking, horse riding and a new canyoning tour, which includes rappelling down a 12m (39ft) waterfall, are also offered.

The office can arrange transfers, which is useful as the *hacienda* is difficult to find. Failing that, a 4WD is definitely recommended!
Patate, near Baños. Tel: Quito office (02) 252 1068, hacienda 098 715 632. www.haciendamanteles.com

Southern Andes
Parque Nacional Podocarpus
Most Ecuadorians consider that the Southern Andes finish at Cuenca and that the Loja and Zamora-Chinchipe provinces are akin to the 'Wild West'. Unsurprisingly then, few tourists venture to this nature-lovers' paradise, which varies from the moody, velvety folds of Loja's mountains to the steamy jungle, waterfalls and rivers at Zamora, a humid town on the edge of the Amazon known as the 'city of birds and

waterfalls'. These two towns, along with Vilcabamba, are entry points to the Parque Nacional Podocarpus.

Named after the podocarpus, Ecuador's only native conifer, found on its velvety green, humid slopes, this large park with numerous climates and habitats stretches from 1,000m to 3,770m (3,280ft to 12,370ft) and ranges from 8°C to 22°C (46°F to 72°F), making it one of the most biodiverse areas in the country. It has 136 lakes, 3,000 to 4,000 plant species, and over 600 bird species, from the toucan to the hummingbird – almost 40 per cent of the country's total. Wildlife ranges from the spectacled bear of the Andes to the tapir of the Amazon.

Entering the park from Loja: The Cajanuma trails on the road to Vilcabamba are popular and lead through cloudforest and *páramo* to spectacular viewpoints. The trail

Walking trail in Podocarpus

signed 'Lagunas del Compadre' leads to 100 stunning glacial lakes, lagoons and ponds.

Maps and information are available in Loja. You can take a taxi to the start of the Cajanuma trail, 13km (8 miles) from Loja, although as it's isolated, it's best to arrange your trip through a tour agency (try Biotours, *see p166*). *Admission charge.*

Entering the park from Zamora: Enter via the 6km-long (4-mile), easy, wide Bombuscaro Trail that runs along the left side of the Bombuscaro River, through lush rainforest, and past natural spas and waterfalls including La Chismosa (The Whispers). With the greatest variety of flora and fauna, it also offers the thrill of tropical showers. Another popular entrance is through the San Francisco Scientific Research Station on the rough road between Loja and Zamora (an adventure in itself), where you'll see podocarpus trees and a variety of birds.

It's a two- to three-hour drive by private car/tour agency from Loja to Zamora. *Admission charge.*

Zaruma

Few tourists take the long, dusty road through barren hills southwest to the isolated colonial town of Zaruma in El Oro (Gold) province. The descendants of Spanish miners who came looking for the Inca kingdom of El Dorado live in this gold-mining town at 1,200m

(3,940ft). Next in line for UNESCO World Heritage status, it has a Wild West feel, with quaint wooden stores selling everything from brooms to bird cages under covered wooden walkways around cobbled streets, and all of it romantically lit at night. It's reputed to have the best coffee in Ecuador, so try it with Zaruma's speciality, *tigrillo* (green banana, egg and cheese) at the unpretentious **El Cafetol** (*112 Bolívar y San Francisco. Tel: (07) 297 2161*).

Things to do include exploring a 500m (1,640ft) disused tunnel at **El Sexmo Tourist Mine**, exploited since the Spanish conquest (*Tel: (07) 297 2666. www.sexmo.net*). Nearby **Hercursa** (*El Sexmo. Tel: (07) 297 3314*) displays unearthed stones and old-fashioned flame lamps still used today. At artesanal mines, like anthills, on **Alborada**, locals eke out a living carrying ore themselves or by mule and

El Sexmo Tourist Mine, Zaruma

A village homestay can be booked through Runa Tupari

extracting it by panning. Nearby are traditional 'Bocadillo' makers such as **Doña Cleme** (*Barrio El Portete, Malvas. Tel: 094 762 466*), who create sugar-cane sweets flavoured with cocoa, guava or coconut.

It's a four-hour journey by taxi from Loja/Vilcabamba (120km/75 miles away) or you can use a Transromeria shared taxi (*Tel: 088 271 384*) to/from Guayaquil (295km/183 miles away).

English-speaking guides are a rarity, but a good choice is **Ramiro Rodríguez** (*Tel: (07) 297 2523 & 092 498 623. Email: kazan_rodriguez@yahoo.com*).

COMMUNITY PROJECTS
Northern Andes
Runa Tupari

To experience how traditional rural Otavaleños live, book a village homestay through successful community-based tour operator Runa Tupari. Guests stay in one of 12 basic but comfortable lodges with families in villages in the Cotacachi region and, outside of eating traditional food with the family, are free to mix as much or as little as they like. Typically, they assist with preparing meals or feeding animals – cutting grass for the precious guinea pigs – when they're not on sightseeing trips during the daytime. Other activities include walks around the village and visits to relatives and friends, collecting milk from those with cows and so on. Families are usually Spanish- and Kichwa-speaking, and, although most visitors get by, some may prefer to be accompanied by a guide. Whichever way you choose to do it, it's a fascinating and enjoyable way to spend time with indigenous people outside the usual touristy experience.

Sucre & Quiroga, opposite Plaza de los Ponchos, Otavalo. Tel: (06) 292 5985 & 097 286 756. www.runatupari.com

Northwestern Andes

Although often bypassed, two special, successful community projects are located in pristine cloudforest near Mindo.

Maquipucuna Reserve

Set in a large cloudforest of outstanding beauty and ranging in altitude from 1,000m to 2,800m (3,280ft to 9,200ft), this reserve hosts some 350 species of birds, including a cock-of-the-rock lek, as well as around 2,000 plant species, 45 mammals and countless butterflies, including the electric-blue morph. The community grows organic vegetables and makes handicrafts out of recycled paper and bamboo. Day visits are possible, and a stop at Yanacocha community is included en route. Accommodation, visits and packages bookable through **Tropic Journeys in Nature** or **Andean Travel Company (ATC)** (*see p127*).

Parroquia Nanegal, 80km (50 miles) northwest of Quito. Tel: (02) 250 7200 & 095 096 666. www.maqui.org. Open: daylight hours. Admission charge.

Santa Lucia Cloudforest Lodge

This off-road, award-winning, community-owned lodge and authentic ecotourism project perched

Cloudforest near Mindo

A rainforest parrot at Yachana Lodge

at 1,900m (6,230ft) is too remote for day visits but offers stays amidst mostly primary cloudforest in the Choco biodiversity hotspot. Some 394 bird species have been recorded here, including a cock-of-the-rock lek. On offer are treks to see birds and waterfalls (and perhaps the elusive puma and spectacled bear who live here) and hikes of up to six days led by indigenous guides.

Barrio la Delicia, Parroquia Nanegal, 80km (50 miles) from Quito and a 90-minute hike from Maquipucuna. Tel: (02) 215 7242.
www.santaluciaecuador.com

Amazon

Yachana Lodge

What distinguishes this award-winning eco-lodge on the Napo River from any other is in its name. 'Yachana' in Kichwa means 'place of learning', and this lodge in a 1,620-hectare (4,000-acre) rainforest reserve is an educational centre recognised by the United Nations World Tourism Organisation as one of the world's best examples of ecotourism. With its focus on community development and cultural experience, Yachana gives visitors the chance to pick and make coffee, try beekeeping, or learn to mould clay pots or weave baskets. The lodge fee goes to help the Napo River communities and train indigenous people in ecotourism. Yachana Jungle Chocolate is also produced from cacao grown here.

Yachana is near the village of Mondaña, three hours by motor canoe from Coca.
Quito office: Vicente Solano E1261 & Avenida Oriental. Tel: (02) 2523 777 and (02) 2503 275. www.yachana.com

When to go

Ecuador's diversity is reflected in its climate, so when to go depends on where you're going. Its varied topography, from Amazon rainforest to Andean cloudforest and from snowy mountain peaks to bare basalt Galápagos Islands, means separate weather patterns, and temperatures relate more to altitude than season, which is essentially either rainy (afternoons) or dry. Andean indigenous Indians don't wear alpaca garments for fashion – roughly speaking, the higher and more exposed, the colder it is.

Ecuador is a year-round destination, but peak tourist season coincides with international and Ecuadorian holidays, namely mid-December to January and June to August. The most interesting local festivals are in June, September and December (*see pp18–19*). Outside of these months, you'll find greater tranquillity, better accommodation rates and availability. Although mainland Ecuador rarely gets overcrowded by Western tourists at any time of year, popular resorts such as Mindo, Papallacta and some coastal resorts get packed with Quiteño weekenders and are best avoided then, if you're searching for tranquillity. International airlines sometimes offer reduced last-minute fares to Ecuador between February and April and in September and October, and it's worth bargaining over hotel prices out of season.

As for activities, climbing is year-round although best in the driest months, December and January. Surfing is best in June–October (south breaks), a time that also offers the best visibility for diving, and December–April (north breaks). Paragliding is best from October to July in the Andes, and in the dry season on the coast.

Andes

In Quito and the northern highlands, the driest months and best mountain views are June–September and December–January. August and September are hottest and October, November and February–mid-April the rainiest. It is often said that Quito can experience all four seasons in just one day! In Cuenca and the southern highlands, the dry season is from August to January, and the rainy season from mid-October to the end of April. Being on the equator, the weather may be spring-like in the lower reaches of the Andes, and it gets cooler the higher the altitude. Quito's temperature range from an average of 10°C (50°F) to 19°C (66°F), whereas Cuenca is a stable average 15°C (59°F).

Amazon

The jungle is hot and humid, with plenty of rainfall year-round. The wettest months are from April to June. Drier months, when canoes may grate along the river floor, are December to March. Daytime temperatures average 25°C (77°F), but can go up to a stifling 32°C (90°F). Nights can be cool.

Pacific Coast

The coast's rainy season and hot months are December to April. May to December is the dry, cooler season, when the weather can be intermittently dreary. Blue skies and the whale-watching season (June–September) unfortunately don't coincide.

Galápagos

In these islands, sea currents determine the season. The warm 'rainy season' is from January to June, but little rain falls on the coast. In the cool, dry season or *garúa* (fine drizzle) from July to December, it's time to don a wetsuit and witness the mist that inspired the Spanish sailors to name the islands 'Las Encantadas' ('Enchanted Isles'). Seas are roughest during August and September. Wildlife can be seen courting and nesting year-round on different islands (*see 'Nature and conservation in the Galápagos', pp112–15*).

WEATHER CONVERSION CHART

25.4mm = 1 inch
°F = 1.8 × °C + 32

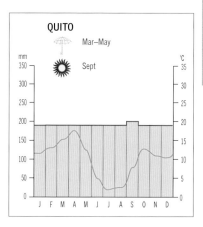

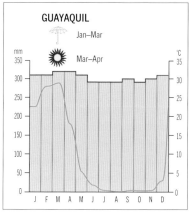

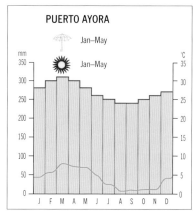

Getting around

Ecuador is a compact country, with many of its attractions a few hours' drive from Quito on good roads, or at most a day's travel. The Panamericana ('Pan-American Highway'), known locally as 'la Pana', is the main transport artery, cutting through the country north to south and well-maintained between Riobamba and Otavalo. Although buses ply this and other main tourist routes, Ecuador's tourism is largely oriented towards excursions and package holidays.

Popular destinations, the Amazon and Galápagos, are reached by a combination of domestic flight (sometimes a six-seater) and cruise boat or canoe. Off the highway, roads can be rough. Even the most popular national park, Cotopaxi, has little infrastructure (being crisscrossed by unsigned dirt roads), facilities, or access by public transport, making a four-wheel drive (needed in some areas), friendly tour guide and packed lunch indispensable. *Haciendas* don't tend to be near a bus stop either. With few directional signs and sometimes dangerous, speedy driving, self-drive isn't recommended, especially for non-Spanish speakers. Travelling by rail is an interesting excursion, rather than a means of transport.

Although the country may be small, it takes around nine hours to drive from Quito to Cuenca, for example, so unless part of a tour, most people use domestic flights as an inexpensive and time-saving option.

By domestic flight

Quito is the domestic flight hub, its airport just 15 minutes' drive from the New Town. Visitors fly from here to the gateway towns of the Amazon, and it takes around 30 minutes to fly to Cuenca, Guayaquil, Loja or Manta. Leave space in your itinerary for delays or cancellation due to weather conditions, which are fairly common. Flights to and from Quito are particularly vulnerable due to its position in a misty valley. Guayaquil is the closer jumping-off point for the Galápagos Islands, so if tight on time, travel from here. The three main carriers are **Tame** (*www.tame.com.ec*), **Aerogal** (*www.aerogal.com.ec*) and **Icaro** (*www.icaro.com.ec*). Tame is the safest and most reliable and is given priority in delays.

Note that many of the routes would be sold as scenic flights in other countries. Tame's dawn flight to Loja offers the best view of the Avenue of Volcanoes, and there are also great

The Avenue of Volcanoes is an amazing sight from the air

views to be had on the trip from Quito to Coca. The lunchtime Emetebe airlines flight from Isabela to Baltra gives a stupendous view of the Galápagos Islands.

By road

Luxury coaches ply the main routes. Tickets need to be bought in advance at towns' and cities' *terminal terrestre* (central bus station). Other road transport includes minibuses, hardy utility vans operating as taxis (the price negotiated in advance) and inexpensive open-air motor taxis (a motorbike with carriage) hopping between towns on the Pacific Coast.

By foot

Ecuador's cities are best seen on foot, intermittently flagging down one of the plentiful, inexpensive (and metered) yellow city cabs. The prefix *Calle* (Street) is often missed off addresses, so that just the name (e.g. *Flores*) is written. Location is usually expressed using the street nearest as reference – *Flores y Chile*, for example.

THE CHIVA

This old-fashioned, colourfully painted, open-sided wooden bus seen countrywide (miniature models in handicraft shops) was originally from the coast. With rooftop room for sacks of grain, fruit and even sheep, chivas traditionally sport bawdy slogans such as 'I like my chicha cold and my girls hot' on the crossbeams. Replicas can be seen in the Andes' Chiva Express (*see pp52–3*). Still used as a public bus, they're also used by tour companies in the Andes for excursions, and Quito celebrates its founding with brass bands playing inside packed chivas.

Riding the Chiva Express is one of the more unusual ways to see the Andes

Countrywide tour operators

Check that tour companies have a 4WD if going to remoter areas. Recommended tour operators are listed below (*see also pp156–73 for regional specialists*).

Andean Travel Company (ATC)

A dynamic, foreign-owned, mid-range tour operator offering countrywide programmes, community tourism and other specialised tours, from archaeology to adventure, to suit every budget.
Edificio CJ, Piso 3, Avenida Amazonas N24-03 & Wilson, Quito.
Tel: (02) 222 8385.
Email: info@andeantc.com

Metropolitan Touring (MT)

Ecuador's biggest tour operator, increasingly specialising in the Galápagos and their own products (such as the Chiva Express) but with the connections to send visitors countrywide.
Avenida de las Palmeras N45-74 & de las Orquídeas, Quito. Tel: (02) 298 8200.
www.metropolitan-touring.com

Surtrek (S)

Highly successful and organised upmarket tour operator with regular and tailormade mainstream or adventurous itineraries countrywide.
Avenida Amazonas 897 & Wilson, Quito. Tel: (02) 250 0660. www.surtrek.com

Tropic Journeys in Nature (T)

Countrywide travel with a conscience with this award-winning ecotourism

PRIVATE GUIDES

An excellent guide who speaks good English (and can drive too) can make or break a trip, some taking you to imaginative places only they know. The following freelance guides are recommended. Most operate around the country (specialist areas are noted below), and can be hired privately or requested through Andean Travel Company (ATC), Metropolitan Touring (MT), Surtrek (S) or Tropic (T) as noted.

Martín Ávila Dynamic, almost native-English-speaker based in Cuenca, but operates countrywide (private company). *Tel: 088 691 724.*

Rodrigo Donoso Enthusiastic Riobamba-based climbing and Chiva Express guide who speaks good English (MT). *Tel: (03) 294 2215 & 099 694 867.*

Alfredo Carrera Friendly, kind, energetic and fun-loving guide with a keen interest in community tourism (ATC). *Tel: 097 070 906.*

Minino Boloña Kind, calm and humorous guide specialising in Isabela (T). *Tel: (05) 252 9008 & 097 871 533.*

Joe Fallowfield Intelligent British but Ecuador-based guide specialising in active adventures (private company). *Tel: 088 590 532. www.ola-adventures.com*

Ricardo Dávila Good-humoured, flexible guide who operates countrywide, with own vehicle (S). *Tel: (02) 261 1304 & 099 284 062.*

Efrain López Good jungle guide (private company). *Tel: (02) 273 2778 & 099 584 571.*

Gustavo Ríos Calm-headed nature and cultural guide (S). *Tel: (02) 229 0352 & 097 597 710.*

operator that specialises in quality natural and cultural experiences.
Edificio Taurus Apartimento 1-A, Avenida República E7-320 & Almagro, Quito. Tel: (02) 222 5907 & (02) 223 4594. www.tropiceco.com

Accommodation

Visitors can experience a wide range of interesting accommodation choices in Ecuador, most in the mid-range category and good value for money. Boutique hotels in colonial mansions await in Quito or Cuenca and in the Andes luxury in nature is found in romantic, antique-filled haciendas *with private grounds, often built on the site of ancient* tambos *('places to rest' in Kichwa). Then there's sleeping in a berth on a luxury Galápagos cruise or on an Amazon riverboat.*

There are also plenty of eco-places to stay countrywide (*see 'Ecotourism in Ecuador', pp82–3*), where remote wood-and-thatch eco-lodges can be surrounded by the buzz of the Amazon rainforest, the romantic mist of the cloudforest or the lapping sea.
More unusual options include staying

Accommodation comes in all materials and sizes

with an indigenous family near Otavalo (*see p120*) or at a community tourism project in the Northwestern Andes, Amazon or Pacific Coast. Quirky finds range from a budget stay in an old station house near Riobamba to catch the *Chiva Express*, to trekking from the strawberry-pink and blue mountain lodge with braided thatch at the foot of Chimborazo owned by Ecuador's greatest living climber. Then there's whale- or howler monkey-watching from an elegant Scandinavian boutique hotel in the teeny coastal village of San Lorenzo, or staying at Chirije, a live archaeological site on a stunning and deserted swimming beach near Bahía de Caráquez.

Book well ahead for Amazon lodges and Galápagos cruises, especially in peak season (June to August and mid-December to January). Hotels also fill up when there's a fiesta, which are very popular locally, and key coastal resorts are busy during public holidays. Places within easy reach of Quito are often booked up with city weekenders, so if you want to avoid noisy crowds, don't stay then.

Most hotels provide bottled or purified water in rooms as an added extra. As Ecuador mainland doesn't receive droves of tourists in many places, hotels are often all-inclusive, offering the best (and often only) restaurant in the area, and providing packed lunches for excursions. Even in the most remote and unlikely places, such as the Amazon, hot showers and flush toilets are found.

The guide *Hospedar* (*Tel: (02) 222 9037. www.tavolaecuador.com*) details the

BOUTIQUE HOTELS OF QUITO

As part of its regeneration, Quito now has a cluster of beautiful boutique hotels. Many are in olde-worlde colonial mansions in the gentle and romantic atmosphere of the historical centre, and a walk away from the city's main attractions. This is a place to enjoy quiet and classic restaurants in the evening. A few new, fashionable boutique hotels have also sprung up in the New Town in the last couple of years, catering to those who prefer modern conveniences, a hot nightlife and closer access to the airport.

100 most characterful accommodation choices across all budgets countrywide (in English and Spanish).

Accommodation

The impressive dining room at Santa Lucia Hotel, Cuenca

Food and drink

Ecuadorians take the adage 'breakfast like a king, lunch like a prince and dine like a pauper' seriously. Lunch is the main meal of the day and great value for visitors – ask for the almuerzo *or* menu del día. *It is often a home-cooked, three-course set meal, usually consisting of soup, main, dessert and juice. Although South American specialities such as* empanadas *(corn pasties filled with meat, vegetables or cheese) are popular, Ecuador has plenty of regional specialities to sample, so look out for* comida típica *on menus.*

Dining out

Eating out is reasonably priced and generally informal. Quito is the country's gastronomic centre. In Inca times, *chasqui* (runners or messengers) brought fish here from the coast, but fishermen now travel up on motorbikes to provide the tuna, shrimp and crab that's made into sushi or served as *ceviche*, a great light lunch.

There is a wide range of drinks available to quench your thirst

Andean specialities include *quimbolitos* (a light, sweetcorn dumpling, wrapped in a leaf) and popular *humitas* (cheese with minced sweetcorn wrapped in the husk and boiled) served warm with coffee or as a light breakfast. Traditional healthy snacks, salted *chocos* (white lupin beans high in calcium) and *tostadas* (toasted maize), are served with drinks. Every type of international food is found here, too, from budget Italian pizzas and American breakfasts to cutting-edge Japanese cuisine. Cuenca's dining scene is a mix of international and traditional, and for the adventurous, it's the place to try roasted *cuy* (guinea pig), also found at stalls in Baños. Alongside shops selling love soups and shamanic herbs in Andean markets, you'll find roasted pigs hanging off hooks or carved on slabs; *hornado* (pork) is a tasty local favourite. Buy fruit here, from indigenous farmers.

Outside of Ecuador's three cities and tourist towns, visitors typically eat at hotel restaurants. *Haciendas* offer the

Roasted guinea pig is popular in Cuenca and is also found at stalls in Baños

best traditional food in the Andes, and eco-lodges provide the best seafood specialities on the coast. Galápagos cruise boats and the Amazon often serve an Ecuadorian-international fusion or mix. Chicken, pork and trout are popular items on menus, but, that said, meat isn't central to the native diet, nor dairy produce, so vegetarians and vegans are easily accommodated with nutritious soups, juices, salads, pulses, corn in the Andes, and a fish or vegetarian option on the better Galápagos boats and in Amazon lodges. Tell *haciendas* in advance, however, as a filet of beef is often the centrepiece of an elegant meal here.

Although tax is 12 per cent and a 10 per cent tip is usually included in restaurant bills, a bit extra for good service is appreciated.

Drinks

A wide variety of delicious and exotic fruit juices (*jugos*) such as the slightly sour *naranjilla*, *mora* (blackberry), *maracuyá* (passionfruit) and *tomate de árbol* (tree tomato) – with more vitamin C than oranges – is found countrywide.

Ecuador imports wine, but the local Pilsener beer is very drinkable. *Aguardiente* (local firewater made from sugar cane) in the Andes is palatable as hot *canelazo* (with cinnamon, sugar, lemon juice and water added).

THE TRIPLE-CARB DINNER

Loosen your belt at local eateries. A side order of rice inexplicably accompanies main dishes – even if that's heaped with noodles or potatoes – and on the coast, fried plantain chips as well.

A taste of Ecuador

Ecuadorian cuisine is wholesome, tasty and as diverse as everything else in the country. Ecuador's garden grows 200 types of Andean potato alone, as well as world-class coffee and cocoa, making some of the planet's best chocolate. Some of the best tuna, shrimp and crab are scooped from its seas, and drinks are made of exotic fruits even seasoned travellers won't have encountered. Regional diversity in the Andes and Pacific Coast combines with cultural influences from every continent to create Ecuador's cuisine. And within the regions, each village, or even *hacienda*, interprets the recipe slightly differently.

The culinary variety and richness of the Americas amazed the 15th-century conquistadors who raved about *palmitos* (palm hearts), avocado, pineapple and fruits such as the tree tomato found here.

Indigenous Indians contributed potatoes (the Incan staple) and corn (referred to as 'the bread of the Indians') to the world larder as well as tomatoes, hot peppers, beans, squash and highly nutritious grains such as *quinoa* (see p61).

The South American Table by Maria Baez Kijac is a good introduction and context to Ecuadorian cuisine, with recipes.

Andes

In the chillier Andes, potatoes and corn still form the basis of the diet. Food tends to be heavy and no meal is complete without a *sopa* (soup), mainly chowders with a regional twist. The most famous is *locro*, a heavy potato soup mixed with *aji* (a paste made from chilli and tree tomato) and mild cheese and topped with avocado and popcorn. With more protein than chicken, *cuy* (guinea pig), an important source of nutrition introduced by the Incas, is a delicacy reserved for fiestas. Oranges and olives, spices such as cumin and saffron brought by Andalusian settlers, the Moorish tradition of using nuts and olive oil, and tapas all influence Andean cooking today.

GASTRONOMY BIBLE

The best 150 restaurants, bars and cafés with a range of food styles, atmospheres and budgets countrywide are detailed in the annual Spanish-language guide *Tavola* (Tel: (02) 222 9037. *www.tavolaecuador.com, website in English*), available for a small charge from many hotels and bookshops.

The fish market, Puerto Ayora

Amazon jungle

Yucca or cassava is the staple food of jungle-dwellers, and unfermented *chicha* is still an important source of nutrition for families. *Chicha*, made from grated yucca in the Amazon and from corn in the Andes and drunk as a source of energy since Inca times, is a highly esteemed drink among Indians. It's traditionally chewed by women to aid fermentation and either drunk immediately or fermented further for one or two days to become potent.

Pacific Coast

Dishes from the coast are lighter – if the ubiquitous fried food is avoided. Ecuadorian *ceviches* (anything from shrimp to spondylus marinated and cooked in lemon juice) are said to be the best in South America. Plantain is popular – *empanadas de verde* made with green plantain dough stuffed with cheese is a speciality – and *patacones* (green plantain chips) are served with everything. Other typical dishes of the region are *cazuelas*, *encocado* and *sopa de Cameron*, all seasoned with coconut milk, peanuts and white or dark sugar, and *bolos de pescado* (fish and peanuts wrapped in banana leaves), which show Asian and Arabic influences.

Entertainment

Entertainment in Ecuador depends on where you visit and is just as diverse as everything else. Nightlife in the Andes might be an elegant dinner, perhaps accompanied by folk music and perhaps a shot of aguardiente *in a* hacienda *followed by a peaceful, early night, or it could be dancing in a salsa club until 3am in the country's capital, Quito. In the Galápagos, entertainment includes lectures on the boat and creating your own party (bring spirits, as drinks aren't included in the price).*

On the Pacific Coast, chilled-out beach bars beckon in surf spots and seafood restaurants in traditional fishing villages. Outside of cities and tourist towns, much of the entertainment is in hotels.

Music plays an important part in Ecuador's bars and clubs

Folklore and culture

Jacchiwa folklore ballet is one of the few cultural shows in Ecuador and is worth seeing. Small clubs called *peñas*, found in Quito and Baños, play live Andean folkloric music. The plazas, such as Santo Domingo in Quito, often have free concerts and shows and are good places to meet local families. Free entertainment is also offered on Guayaquil's Malecón 2000, and the city also has one of South America's largest IMAX cinemas. For theatre, cinemas and music in Quito, check listings in the *El Comercio* newspaper; seeing the National Symphony costs just a dollar. The best cultural experience in Ecuador, however, has to be attending a festival. Choose from city celebrations of independence, the traditional indigenous fiestas in the Andes, or the wild and famously colourful Mama Negra in Latacunga.

Nightlife

Quito is the nightlife centre of Ecuador, offering everything from swanky

Musicians are a common sight in Ecuador and help to create a convivial atmosphere

restaurants to bohemian bars with live jazz and salsa clubs in its Mariscal District. Plaza Foch (Mariscal Foch & Reina Victoria) is the epicentre, spilling over with eateries, cafés and bars, with regular concerts and cultural events held in one corner. Quito has a fabulous gastro scene, too, with everything from Ecuadorian fusion in Zazu to international cuisine, whether top-notch Japanese or authentic pizza. Ecuadorians are late-night party-goers, and the weekend starts on Thursday. The party doesn't get started until around 11pm and bars are open until 3am.

The nightlife in the party town of Baños is concentrated in the bars and clubs on Calle Eloy Alfaro. Further south, Café Eucalyptus is the top nightspot in Cuenca, with live music nightly. Montañita and Canoa on the Pacific Coast have a laid-back, surf-party, bars-on-the-beach scene, while Puerto Ayora in the Galápagos offers everything from live music at gastro-pub The Rock to traditional coastal specialities eaten al fresco from stalls along Calle de los Kioskos.

Entertainment for locals is centred in the plazas and around family activities in the provinces.

THE RHYTHM OF THE NIGHT

Even if you're no party animal and just want peace and quiet on your holiday, you may find it difficult to avoid all forms of lively nightlife; the sound of cockerels may be heard in 'quiet' small towns and village homestays, and in the jungle the strange gurgle of howler monkeys and a million insects will serenade you well into the wee hours. Even on Galápagos boats, the sound of the engine can be heard below deck, as most travelling is done at night.

Shopping

Ecuador's shopping is as diverse as its culture and nature, with traditional handicrafts the main buy. These include the famous Panama hats weaved from the fine straw found at the coast, textiles including jumpers, scarves and ponchos made from Andean alpaca wool, filigree jewellery produced from silver and gold mined around Cuenca, animal figures carved from tagua *(vegetable ivory) found on the coast and jungle, and the exports chocolate and coffee.*

The most fun shopping is to be had at lively local Indian markets, but the best quality pieces are found in crafts villages and in shops and galleries in the main cities. Shops and galleries won't support local families directly, however, so if you want to support families as well as get fine-quality purchases, crafts villages across the Andes are the best places to shop.

Andes

Saturday's colourful market in Otavalo is the place to bargain for a wide range of handicrafts. Other Andean markets, such as Salasaca, also have a handicrafts section (*see p59*).

Quito

The capital has one-stop shopping, mostly in the Mariscal district in the New Town. For inexpensive handicrafts, try the **mini Otavalo market** in El Ejido Park opposite the Hilton Colón at weekends (and Mondays, Wednesdays and Fridays in July and August); on Sundays, local artists sell paintings from the railings. Prices are fixed but reasonable at the handicraft alleys in the daily **Market Artisanal** (*Juan León Mera & Reina Victoria*).

Pretty glassware and ceramics are made in Quito. **Galeria Latina** (*Juan León Mera N23-69. Tel: (02) 254 0380*) sells quality handicrafts, and the contemporary jeweller **Christian Quintero** has branches in JW Marriott and the Swissôtel (*Avenida 12 de Octubre & Cordero. Tel: (02) 250 2282. www.christianquintero.com*). On the streets surrounding Avenida Amazonas is the famous English-language bookshop **Libri Mundi** (*Hermano Miguel 8-14 & Mariscal Sucre. Tel: (02) 284 3783*), the **Hyla Shop** (*Juan León Mera & Roca*) with a great range of quality T-shirts with cool logos, and **Tatoo** (*Juan León Mera 820 & Wilson. Tel: (02) 290 4533*), Ecuador's own quality outdoor clothing brand.

Fairtrade original handicrafts can be bought at **Museo Mindalae** (*Reina*

Traditional Tigua paintings at a market in Otavalo

Victoria & La Niña, Mariscal. Tel: (02) 255 5394) or in the Centro Histórico at **Tianguez** (*Plaza de San Francisco. Tel: (02) 223 0609*). Traditional craftsmanship is found at **Escuela Taller** (*Montufar N2-50 & Pereira. Tel: (02) 295 9325*), and for coffee and chocolate visit **Camari** (*Marchena Oe2-38 & Versalles. www.camari.org*). Particularly exquisite handicrafts are found in **Folklore Olga Fisch** (*Avenida Colón E10-53. Tel: (02) 254 1315. www.olgafisch.com*), which has branches in the Hilton Colón and Patio Andaluz.

Northern villages

Excellent-quality handmade products from alpaca jumpers to woollen wall hangings are a fair fixed price at **El Gran Condor** (*Plaza Central.*

Tel: (06) 269 0161. www. artesaniaelgrancondor.com) in Peguche. In Cotacachi, the leather capital of Ecuador, shops selling everything from belts to handbags and suitcases line Calle 10 de Agosto where a leather market is held on Sundays. For quality products at a reasonable price, try **La Curtiembre** (*10 de Agosto 11-61. Tel: (06) 291 5910*).

In Tigua the son of the artist Alfredo Toaquiza and other relatives run the village co-operative **Galería Tigua** (*Main Road. Tel: (03) 281 4868 & 099 343 969*), selling the best-quality indigenous Tigua paintings at the same prices as at markets, along with painted jewellery boxes and alder masks. Further south, distinctive, fine wall-hangings sporting animal, bird and

Cotacachi is famed for its leather goods

plant motifs can be bought at handicraft stalls (best on Sundays) in the town square in Salasaca village near Baños, or, better still, at family homes.

Cuenca

Cuenca is the centre of Panama hat production and ceramics as well as Ikat weave and filigree jewellery. Shopping here is in artisanal shops in the Centro Histórico, such as **El Tucán** (*Gran Colombia 7-60. Tel: (07) 283 4386*) and **Spondylus** (*Gran Colombia 20-85. Tel: (07) 282 0689*), which specialises in jewellery made from the sacred shell. **Homero Ortega & Hijos** (*Avenida Gil Ramirez Davalos 3-86. Tel: (07) 780 9000. www.homeroortega.com*) is Ecuador's most famous Panama hat producer. **Taller E Vega** (*just below Mirador de Turi. Tel: (07) 288 1407*) is the workshop of the celebrated ceramicist Eduardo Vega.

Southern villages

A fairtrade excursion to outlying villages includes Sigsig, where Panama hats are found for reasonable prices at the weaving co-operative **Asociación de Mujeres Tejedoras María Auxiliadora** on the road to Gualaquiza. Gualaceo is known for Ikat textile weaving; woollen and silk shawls and scarves are still made on back-strap looms, some using natural dyes. Shop at José Jimenez's **Ikat Taller Artesanal** (*on the road to Gualaceo, 1km from Puente Europa. Tel: 05 699 163*) or at private addresses that can only be provided by your guide.

Chordeleg produces filigree jewellery, mostly in silver, sold along with other handicrafts in around 25 shops lining the main square José María Vargas and Calle Juan Bautista Cobos. Try **Joyeria Puerto del Sol**. Note that some shops in this village are only open at weekends.

Pacific Coast
Montecristi

It's worth the trip here, to the place where the Panama hats with the finest weave are finished, to buy a well-priced, good-quality hat. Stalls are found on Calle Eloy Alfaro in the wooden **Museo des Artesanías**. For quality hats at a

Market day in Montecristi

A woman spins wool in Peguche to prepare it for weaving

reasonable price, try **Alfran** opposite (*Eloy Alfaro & 23 de Octubre. Tel: (05) 231 0854*).

Galápagos Islands

As the use of natural products in the national park is restricted, Galapageno handicrafts are few and far between. The main shopping stop is Puerto Ayora, Santa Cruz. Its main drag, Avenida Charles Darwin, is lined with shops selling handicrafts from the mainland and stalls selling T-shirts emblazoned with slogans such as 'I love Boobies'. Tasteful T-shirts are found at the **National Park Store** (*near Charles Darwin Research Station, Avenida Charles Darwin. Open: Mon–Sat 8am–noon & 3–6pm*). There's also a branch of the well-priced outdoor clothing store **Tatoo**.

Note that if you want to buy crafts from mainland Ecuador, they're a third of the price on the mainland itself.

ALL IN THE WEAVE

A good Panama hat can be judged by its weave. Check it by holding it up to the light; the less light shining through the weave, the better quality the hat.

Unique things to buy on the islands include carved animals (from hammerhead sharks to sea lions) – the prettiest in wood – and Galapageno coffee, reputedly the best in Ecuador. For something original, **Reflections** (*Avenida Charles Darwin & Bolívar Naveda. Tel: (08) 536 3634*) sells crafts made by Galapagenos as well as tasteful crafts from elsewhere. **Galería Aymara** (*Avenida Charles Darwin & Los Piqueros. Tel: (05) 252 6835. www.galeria-aymara.com*) has an exquisite selection of Latin American art and jewellery, although at Western prices, and the ultra-feminine **Angelique Art Gallery** (*Tel: (05) 252 6656. www.sarah-darling.com*) has silk-screen cushions, paintings and handmade cards.

ome pieces of jewellery are made from spondylus, used as currency in ancient times

Sport and leisure

With its diversity of ecosystems, Ecuador offers an astounding array of active adventure. This ranges from some of the planet's best diving, found in the Galápagos Islands, to 62 Andean summits to climb and, with half of the country crisscrossed with Amazon rivers, plenty of white water for rafting and kayaking. The wild Andean páramo *makes for great horse riding, and trekking possibilities are endless. Unusually, challenges for the experienced are offered alongside great options for beginners.*

Climbing

Ecuador has more than enough challenging peaks to attract serious climbers and a good variety of easily accessible peaks for beginners, too. The most popular and safest is Cotopaxi, which, six hours to the summit and three down, can be climbed by most averagely fit people – with proper acclimatisation and instruction (*see p163*).

For more challenging climbing, including glacial climbing with ice picks and crampons, smaller summits are used as acclimatisation before higher peaks and technical climbs are tackled. On a two-week trip, it's possible to climb Pichincha, Ilinizas North, Cotopaxi and the country's highest peak, Chimborazo.

Rock climbing is also popular, with over 200 climbing routes around Cuenca and, in Guayaquil, one of the largest artificial climbing walls in South America. A Via Ferrata with rappelling and zipline is at Hacienda Santa Rita near Cotopaxi National Park (*see p163*).

Diving and snorkelling

The Galápagos Islands are considered one of the seven underwater wonders of the world, and hammerhead sharks are a main dive attraction. Diving ranges from PADI courses to day trips from Santa Cruz (*see p101*) to world-class dive cruises to Darwin and Wolf. Other great dive sites are found off Isla de la Plata in Machalilla National Park.

Snorkelling is an important aspect of a Galápagos cruise and a good way to

---

CLIMBING HEROES

Englishman Edward Whymper was the first person to climb Chimborazo, in 1880. He climbed ten peaks in Ecuador, eight previously unclimbed.

Ecuador's most famous living climber is Marco Cruz. He first climbed Chimborazo when he was 13 and has now climbed it over 600 times (*see Expediciones Andinas, pp164–5, & Suggested reading and media, p150*).

see turtles, sea lions and plenty of rainbow-coloured fish.

Horse riding

Ecuador is a great place to play cowboy (or girl) in the Andes, where the *chagra* or cowboy culture still thrives. Adapted to the altitude, horses here start breathing heavily before they start to climb (so don't think yours will expire) and are sure-footed along the often rocky paths.

Every stage and age is catered for in Ecuador, from paddock rides for toddlers (*see pp146–7*) to half- or full-day rides from many Andean *haciendas* and week-long trips led by specialists for beginners or advanced (*see pp160, 163 & 165–6*). Make sure you acclimatise, as *páramo* means altitudes of up to 4,000m (13,125ft).

Experienced riders may want to time their visit with the monthly rodeo (excluding April and May) at **Hacienda Yanahurco** in Cotopaxi in the Central Andes (*Tel: (02) 244 5248. www.haciendayanahurco.com*). Trips can be organised through *haciendas* such as La Alegria and El Porvenir, or tour operator Ride Andes. Those with a sense of adventure may venture on horseback up a live volcano on Galápagos' Isabela Island.

Motorcycling

Ecuador's tracks for motorcross, hare scramble and enduro have been designed to international standards and have hosted international competitions. Motorcycling routes include Mitad del Mundo to Bahía de Caráquez on the coast.

n horseback at Chimborazo

With its many pristine rivers and spectacular scenery, Ecuador is a delight for white-water tubing

Mountain biking

Plenty of opportunities exist for mountain biking in Ecuador, such as beginners' cross-country, nature trails such as the back road from Quito to Mindo (*see* The Biking Dutchman, *p159*) and the road to Patate around Baños, cycling from Puerto López to Agua Blanca on the Ruta del Sol on the Pacific Coast (*see pp94–5*) or even through Isabela's wetlands on the Galápagos Islands (*see pp110–11*), and advanced cycling down volcanoes in the Andes (*see* Tierra del Volcán, *p163*), with descents of over 3,000m (9,850ft). Bike hire is available in Quito and Baños, and tour agencies offer imaginative guided cycle rides.

Paragliding

Cruz Loma at Quito's Volcán Pichincha is the place to paraglide over the city, and on the coast Canoa is a popular spot to learn.

Surfing

Ecuador hosted the World Surfing Games in Salinas in 2004 and its many beach breaks and point breaks come from Pacific Ocean storms. World-class surfing is found near Puerto Baquerizo Moreno, San Cristóbal Island and the fishing village of San Mateo, near Manta on the Pacific Coast. Montañita and Canoa are both famous surf towns and good places to learn to surf.

Trekking

Ecuador offers a wide variety of trekking options, many in remote regions where it's just you and the birds. Trails in national parks vary from being well marked with maps and information and even a visitors' centre (e.g. Cotopaxi, El Cajas and Podocarpus) to being completely off the tourist trail (e.g. Llanganates National Park near Baños and Sangay).

Imaginative treks are informally offered through smaller recommended local agencies, freelance guides, eco-lodges or on the private lands of *haciendas*. The country's most popular long trek is the Inca Trail (*see pp72–3*).

Andean lake treks are favourites. From Laguna Quilotoa through the Río Toachi Canyon to Chugchilán is one of the best day walks, arranged through the Black Sheep Inn (*see p161*). The walk around Laguna Cuicocha (*see pp42–3*) near Otavalo is stunning and varied, as is the circuit around Laguna Toreadora in El Cajas National Park in the Southern Highlands.

White-water rafting and kayaking

With one of the world's highest concentrations of rivers per square kilometre, Ecuador has hundreds of kilometres of world-class white water, of varying grades of difficulty. With some of the largest, warmest and most pristine rivers winding through spectacular gorges, canyons, valleys and jungle to feed into the Amazon River,

Tena has become known as the country's white-water rafting and kayaking capital, with class IV+ rapids on the Río Misahualli for the experienced. It hosted the World Rafting Championship 2005. Nearer Quito, the Río Toachi and Río Blanco offer class III rapids. White-water rafting is also popular in Baños, but make sure you choose a trusted operator as accidents have happened there.

Sea kayaking off the Pacific Coast and Galápagos Islands is also popular, and offered off cruise boats, although the national park authorities have recently tightened the Galápagos Islands' laws.

Trekking in the Cordillera range of the Andes

Children

Ecuador is not known as a family-friendly destination, but like most Latin American countries, being family-focused themselves means Ecuadorians welcome children. This affects the bottom line. Children under 12 go half-price on flights (not long-distance buses), get accommodation discounts and can order half portions in restaurants. Tour companies have special child-friendly packages, which are the easiest ways to get around, but families can travel quite safely by public transport as well.

Hotels don't typically have babysitting services (kids' clubs are unimaginable) and, if available, babysitters don't usually speak English. However, learning some Spanish as a family will open doors to experiences with locals, so consider learning some before you go or at a school on arrival. Pick up a copy of the local comic, *Condorito*, to help.

Families with young children can follow the example of Quiteño families and head to the coastal beaches in season or the hot springs at Papallacta (*see box opposite*). Children of age eight upwards may get more out of the many nature- and wildlife-based activities at the latter. Thrills for young teenagers include white-water rafting, canopy

Small towns are a good place to meet friendly local children

Llamas at Hacienda La Alegria

FAMILY-FRIENDLY ADVENTURE

The following are listed in detail in the Directory (*pp156–73*).

1 **Hacienda La Alegria, Northern Andes**
Close to Quito by road or *Chiva Express* (a fun ride for older children), with llamas to pet and activities designed for families.

2 **Finch Bay Hotel, Santa Cruz, Galápagos**
Offers a flexible, land-based package with walks, a swimming hole, giant tortoises, lava tubes, a beach nearby and day trips by boat to nearby islands.

3 **Termas de Papallacta, Amazon's edge**
Informal and friendly hot springs in mountain scenery, with family cabins set away from the main resort and shallow pools safe for supervised toddlers.

4 **White-water tubing, Mindo, Northwestern Andes** Taking an inner tube down the Río Mindo is great fun for young teenagers, and canopy rides are also found here.

5 **Jungle Lodge, Amazon** Sani or Yachana Lodge are family-friendly Amazon options for older children. As well as spotting wildlife and going on canoe rides, there are chances to learn weaving and use blowpipes.

6 **Isla de la Plata** This 'mini Galápagos' off the Pacific Coast is easier and cheaper to get to than the main islands, with family-friendly lodges and trekking (among other things) offered nearby. Older children can see exotic seabirds and spot whales from June to September.

rides and climbing, cycling and horse riding. For mixed ages, a family-friendly, working *hacienda* in the Andes is a good bet. These are destinations in themselves, with lots of room to run around, animals, activities and excursions, some to the colourful Otavalo market. Another good alternative is a family homestay, where children can play with local children and get involved in anything from cooking to feeding guinea pigs.

Transport delays are common, so keep your itinerary simple and carry snacks – packets of banana chips and dried fruit are sold here. The many flavoured fresh fruit drinks (check pure water is used) should be a hit with children and they may even be persuaded to eat soups; in the Andes popcorn and avocado are often sprinkled on top. Chicken and chips and suchlike are on standby if children have difficulty with Ecuadorian cuisine, and European or American-owned establishments may be able to be food-flexible. Note that documentary evidence of parental responsibility must be carried when entering and leaving Ecuador.

Essentials

Arriving and departing

Ecuador can be visited as part of an overland South America trip, most commonly accessed by road from Peru in the south or reached along the Amazon river highway from Brazil as part of a river cruise. Most people arrive by air, however, into the two main international airports: Quito's **Mariscal Sucre** (*www.quitoairport.com*) or Guayaquil's recently built **José Joaquín de Olmedo** (*tel: (04) 216 9209; www.aag.org.ec*). All flights stop in Quito first.

By air

Non-direct flights from the UK are with **KLM** (*www.klm.com*), **Iberia** (*www.iberia.com*), **American Airlines** (*www.aa.com*) or **Continental** (*www.continental.com*) and take 15–17 hours to Quito. American Airlines, Continental and **LanChile** (*www.lan.com*) fly direct from Houston and New York, taking 5–7 hours. American Airlines from Toronto and Montreal connecting through Miami is the best bet for Canadians, taking $7^1/_2$ hours, or Canadian Airlines via the US if you're not based in those cities. Flight time from Australia and New Zealand is 25–27 hours, with non-direct routes with **Qantas** (*www.qantas.com.au*) and LanChile via Santiago from Sydney. New Zealanders can connect with this or travel via Buenos Aires with **Aerolineas Argentinas** (*www.aerolineas.com.ar*). It takes around 19 hours to fly from South Africa via other South American cities.

Customs

Visitors can bring up to US$1,250 worth of items for personal use and up to 2 litres of alcoholic drinks and 200 cigarettes. It is illegal to take home ancient artefacts.

Electricity

Domestic power supply is 110/120 volts. Plugs have two US-compatible flat-pronged pins. Visitors from other countries should bring an adaptor, or buy in cities here.

Internet

One terminal with broadband connection is found in most mid-range hotels (apart from remote Amazon lodges), with wireless increasingly available. Inexpensive Internet cafés are found in cities and tourist areas, the most famous being **Papayanet** (*Caluma & Juan León Mera, Mariscal, Quito. Tel: (02) 225 6574. www. papayanet.com.ec. Open: 7am–1am*).

Money

Ecuador changed its currency to the US dollar in 2000 and both Ecuadorian and US notes and coins are used interchangeably. Bring small notes as change is often scarce and US$50 and US$100 bills may be viewed suspiciously. Credit cards are often difficult to use here and traveller's cheques not always easy to change, but ATMs are found in towns and cities everywhere. Use those in hotels and shopping centres for extra security.

Opening hours
Most shops and businesses open weekdays 9am–1pm and 2.30–6.30pm. Banks and other businesses, including museums, usually open weekdays 9am–5pm and Saturdays 10am–noon. Ecuador is traditionally religious, and many places therefore close on Sunday. Also note that shops, attractions and even evening venues are sometimes only open Thur–Sun, as they cater specifically to the local weekend market.

Passports and visas
An entry stamp on arrival guarantees a stay of up to 90 days for British, US, Canadian, Australian, New Zealand and South African citizens. Make sure passports are valid for at least six months from the time of your arrival.

Pharmacies
Fybeca pharmacy has branches all over Ecuador and, although prescription medication needs to be brought from home, it can supply travellers' general needs.

Post
Postal reliability from the *correos* is variable. International courier companies Fedex and DHL are reliable but expensive.

Some services can be quite basic, such as the main post office in Isabela

Pick up a good map before visiting remote locations such as Chugchilán

Public holidays
1 Jan New Year's Day
Feb/Mar Carnival
Mar/Apr Good Friday (Holy Week)
1 May Labour Day
24 May Battle of Pichincha
26 May Simón Bolívar's birthday
10 Aug Independence Day
9 Oct Guayaquil Independence Day
2 Nov All Souls' Day
3 Nov Cuenca Independence Day
6 Dec Founding of Quito
25 Dec Christmas Day
31 Dec New Year's Eve

Smoking
Smoking is allowed in public places including restaurants, bars and shops.

Suggested reading and media
Ecuador, Chagras: Ecuador's Andean Cowboys, Spirit of the Huaorani and *Galápagos: The Untamed Isles* are four beautifully produced coffee-table books containing images by locally based photographer Pete Oxford (*www.peteoxford.com*), often on display at hotels and purchasable only within the country.
Mountains of Ecuador by Marco Cruz, the country's climbing pioneer.
The Panama Hat Trail by Tom Miller and Tony Hillerman, for entertaining and insightful social history.
Savages by Jo Kane, dealing with the Huaorani struggle to preserve their way of life.
Galápagos: The Islands That Changed The World by Paul D Stewart, and *Galápagos: A Natural History* by John Krichner are two of the best companions on an island trip.

Useful websites
www.ecuador.com
www.hipecuador.com
www.thisisecuador.com
www.exploringecuador.com
www.ecuadorexplorer.com
www.goecuador.com
www.thebestofecuador.com
www.ecuador-travel-guide.org

Useful organisations
Ministry of Tourism Branches countrywide, provides maps, advice and information.
Eloy Alfaro N32-300 & Carlos Tobar, Quito. Tel: (2) 250 7555.
www.purecuador.com,
www.ecuador.travel &
www.turismo.gov.ec

Tax
An additional fee of 12 per cent VAT and 10 per cent service is added in most hotels and restaurants. International airport tax is cheaper if flying from Guayaquil instead of Quito.

Telephones
The two main local providers of phone services are **Movistar** (lime green and blue) and **Porta** (red). These offer public phone booths throughout the country in which their phone cards may be used. Overseas mobiles won't work here unless they are a quad band phone or unlocked to receive a local SIM card. Call home from one of the ubiquitous *cabinas* – Pacifictel or Andinatel are the cheapest.
The international dialling code for Ecuador is 593. Mobile prefixes are 09 or 08.

City codes:
Baños *03*
Cuenca *07*
Galápagos *05*
Guayaquil *04*
Otavalo *06*
Puerto López *05*
Quito *02*

Time
Ecuador Mainland Time is –5 hours GMT (the same as US Eastern Standard Time) and –6 GMT (one hour behind US EST) on the Galápagos Islands. The country doesn't observe daylight saving.

Toilets
Toilets are usually signed *hombres* (men) and *mujeres* (women) (sometimes, confusingly, H and M). 'C' on taps doesn't stand for cold as at home, but *caliente* (hot in Spanish). 'F' (*fria*) signals the cold tap. As toilet paper blocks the small pipes, the custom is to throw used toilet tissue into an adjacent bin (often without a lid). Take toilet paper or tissues around with you or risk being caught short. Public toilets often don't have any.

Travellers with disabilities
Ecuador has limited infrastructure for disabled travellers on a budget, as the best facilities are found in international hotels. Getting in a canoe to an Amazon lodge, getting off a *panga* onto the shore and navigating uneven terrain in cities are not conducive to the wheelchair-bound. However, travellers with disabilities will be welcomed and touched by the kindness and helpfulness of Ecuadorian people. For general advice and help, visit *www.globalaccessnews.com*

Language

Spanish and Kichwa (the language of the Incas, spoken by around a fifth of the population) are Ecuador's official languages. Other indigenous languages are spoken in isolated areas, such as the Amazon. Spanish is the common language of communication and the accent in Ecuador is easy to understand. Most people working in tourism speak English, but as not much English is spoken on the street, it definitely helps to learn some of the language. For extra help, check out *www.studyspanish.com*, an excellent free online tutorial. Speaking a few phrases of Kichwa, which the Spanish never succeeded in eradicating, will go far, especially in Andean markets and villages. Sign up for Kichwa lessons in Quito at *www.kichwas.com*

SPANISH

English	Spanish (pronunciation)
yes	*sí* (see)
no	*no* (no)
please	*por favor* (por favoor)
thank you (very much)	*(muchas) gracias* (mOOchaas GRAseeaz)
you're welcome	*de nada* (de NAAda)
hello	*hola* (oeLAH)
good day/morning	*buenos días* (BWEnas DEEyas)
good afternoon	*buenas tardes* (BWEnas TARdes)
good evening	*buenas noches* (BWEnas NOCHes)
goodbye/see you later	*adios* (adeeYOS)/*hasta luego* (hAsTa LewAYgoe)
excuse me	*perdón* (pearDON)
sorry	*lo siento* (loe seeYENtoe)
where?	*¿donde?* (donday)
when?	*¿cuando?* (KWANdo)
why?	*¿porque?* (porKAY)
how?	*¿como?* (comow)
room	*habitación* (habitASyon)
beach	*playa* (plEYEer)
church	*iglesia* (igLAYsya)

how much?	*¿cuanto?* (KWANtow)
the bill	*la cuenta* (la cEWENta)
do you speak English?	*¿habla usted inglés?* (aablah Oostead eenGLAYS)
I don't understand	*no entiendo* (no enteeYENdoe)
I'm hungry	*tengo hambre* (tengo AMBray)
I'm thirsty	*tengo sed* (tengo SAYd)
bon appetit	*buen provecho* (BWEn ProVECHoe)
pretty	*lindo* (LEEndoe)
beautiful	*bonito* (bonEEtoe)

KICHWA

English	Kichwa
yes	*ari*
no	*mana*
hello	*imanalla*
see you later	*asha kashkaman*
please	*jau man*
thank you (very much)	*pagui (shungulla)*
how are you?	*imanalla kangui?*
I'm fine	*allillami kapani*
where are you from?	*maymanda kangui?*
I am from	*manda kani*
my name is	*nuka shuti mikan*

¿HABLA ESPAÑOL?

Quito is the language capital of Ecuador, the most popular centre for learning Spanish in South America. About 80 schools offer group or private tuition at inexpensive rates. Most provide family stays, activities and excursions. Among those recommended by the **South American Explorers Club** (*www.saexplorers.org*) are:

Amazonas
Large, established school with use of facilities at the Hilton Colón.
718 Jorge Washington & Amazonas, Rocafuerte Washington Block, 2nd/3rd floor.
Tel: (02) 250 4654 & (02) 252 7509. www.eduamazonas.com

Bipo & Toni
Good teachers and a lovely school that donates to environmental projects.
Carrion & Leónidas Plaza. Tel: (02) 254 7090. www.bipo.net

Emergencies

Emergency numbers

Police *101*
Fire *102*
Medical emergency *911* (main cities)

Health care

Comprehensive health insurance is recommended, covering any planned activities and perhaps evacuation cover. Two hospitals in Quito have 24-hour emergency service and English-speaking doctors, but good medical treatment is not always available outside main cities.

Typhoid, tetanus, diphtheria, hepatitis A and yellow fever vaccinations are recommended and malaria prophylaxis if visiting the Amazon or Pacific Coast. Even so, it's essential to cover up, as there has been

Be careful when buying from street stalls

ADAPTING TO THE ALTITUDE

Dizziness, headaches, breathlessness, tiredness and nausea are caused by the altitude. Drinking lots of water, reducing alcohol intake and taking it easy for the first few days helps. Coca leaf teabags or *zunfo*, the Ecuadorian equivalent, are good for combatting the symptoms and are available at hotels and restaurants on request. For a low-altitude trip, see 'Suggested itineraries' (*pp22–5*).

an increase in reported cases of mosquito-borne dengue fever. Locally available Detan repellent works and some swear by a course of Vitamin B complex. Bugs are most often brought into beds via outdoor clothes. Better lodges and hotels fumigate or spray rooms during dinner.

Stomach upsets usually occur from eating in cheaper restaurants or street stalls and markets or from unpurified water added to fruit drinks – ask before ordering if unsure. Bottled water *con gas* (sparkling) or *sin gas* (still) are bought cheaply countrywide. Many establishments offer filtered water that is safe to drink and it reduces plastic waste.

In the dry, dusty Andes, visitors may experience irritation with contact lenses, so plan for limited wear.

And whatever you do, don't underestimate the power of the equatorial sun. Lather on sunscreen, even if there's cloud cover.

Safety and crime

Outside border areas, Ecuador is arguably one of the safest countries in South America, but it's poor, so take sensible precautions. Keep an eye on belongings in cities in areas with a high concentration of tourists and don't wander alone, even as a group, in remote places: rapes and armed robberies, although rare, have been reported. Historical centres are best visited with a local or guide, and only use registered taxis. Political demonstrations are commonplace, and on occasion turn violent.

Although most visits pass without incident, beware of strangers offering food, drinks, leaflets, telephone cards or cigarettes which may contain the drug 'scopolamine'. Ideal for thieves, it sedates victims and causes amnesia. 'Express kidnappings' have been reported in Guayaquil and the south, the victims being held until money is extracted using their bank cards.

Erupting volcanoes are best watched from a distance, and check activity in volatile areas before travelling. Amazon adventures are usually trouble-free, but the jungle is no holiday park: be careful!

The main tourist centres of cities and areas such as Mitad del Mundo have a noticeable but friendly and helpful police presence. The tourist police can be reached in Quito by telephone (*Tel: (02) 254 3983*).

Visit *www.fco.gov.uk/ knowbeforeyougo* for full information on political and safety issues.

Embassies and consulates

For any serious trouble (e.g. if you are involved in an accident or lose your passport), contact your embassy or consulate in Quito. Lone travellers may wish to register on arrival, for extra safety. New Zealand and South Africa don't have representation in Ecuador, but Australians can use the Canadian Embassy.

Canada/Australia *Avenida 6 de Diciembre 2816 & Paul Rivet. Tel: (02) 223 2114. www.quito.gc.ca*

UK *Naciones Unidas & Avenida República de El Salvador. Tel: (02) 297 0800. www.britishembassy.gov.uk/Ecuador*

US *12 de Octubre & Patria. Tel: (02) 256 2890. http://ecuador.usembassy.gov*

Be sure you know your way back to base when hiking in the wilderness

Directory

Accommodation price guide

A scale of one to four stars has been used as a price guide, with one star indicating the cheapest option and four stars the most expensive. Prices are in US$ per person sharing a double room, although hotel rates are often quoted per room rather than per person. Tax, high at 22 per cent (10 per cent service, 12 per cent VAT), is excluded from prices. Breakfast is usually included in the price for three stars and above. Where full board is offered, and this is sometimes obligatory due to remoteness or as part of the experience, a note is made, but rates are calculated to include just breakfast, for ease of comparison.

When booking accommodation remember that a *matrimonial* is a double bed, whereas a *doble* means a room with twin beds.

★	up to $50
★★	$50–$100
★★★	$100–$200
★★★★	over $200

Eating out price guide

The eating out price guide is based on the average price of a meal for one person without drinks or service. Prices are in US$.

Note that restaurants of two stars and above quote their prices without taxes, so expect an extra 22 per cent to be added to the bill.

★	up to $10
★★	$10–$20
★★★	$20–$30
★★★★	over $40

QUITO

ACCOMMODATION

La Casa Sol ★

This bright orange edifice is a friendly 'Andean hostel' run by indigenous Otavaleños and scattered with indigenous art and artefacts.

Calama 127 & 6 de Diciembre. Tel: (02) 223 0798. www.lacasasol.com

Café Cultura ★★

White colonial mansion in the New Town with an informal, friendly atmosphere and loads of character. En-suite rooms are individually decorated by artists, with painted frescoes and furniture; room 1 has a romantic sunken bath. Guests hang out on leather couches in the wood-panelled library and a cosy restaurant

with stone fireplace serves eclectic bistro-style cuisine.
Calle Robles & Reina Victoria.
Tel: (02) 222 4271 & (02) 250 4078 & (02) 256 4956.
www.cafecultura.com

Casa Aliso ★★★
This 'small luxury home', on a quiet street near to the Mariscal, has ten en-suite rooms romantically decorated in classic style with marble bathrooms and a divine bed. Some have manicured private gardens.
Francisco Salazar E12-137 & Toledo, Floresta.
Tel: (02) 252 8062.
www.casaliso.com

Le Parc Hotel ★★★
Opened in 2007, this contemporary boutique hotel has a water moat in the lobby, zebra-print coffee tables, stand-alone bathtubs and rooftop terrace bar.
Avenida República de El Salvador N34-349 & Irlanda. Tel: (02) 227 6800.
www.leparc.com.ec

Patio Andaluz ★★★
Quito's first boutique hotel, this lovingly restored 16th-century colonial mansion is paces from attractions in the Centro Histórico. Small and personal, it has 31 traditionally decorated suites, romantic dining in the inner courtyard and an exclusive Olga Fisch boutique.
Avenida García Moreno N6-52.
Tel: (02) 228 0830. www. hotelpatioandaluz.com

Villa Colonna ★★★
An exquisitely tasteful six-room B&B with a rooftop terrace in a colonial mansion where guests are looked after with fine attention to detail. Non-smoking, adults only.
Benalcázar 1128 & Esmeraldas.
Tel: (02) 295 5805.
www.villacolonna.ec

Hacienda Chillo-Jijón ★★★★
Gloved servers await in the grand dining room of this lavish and personal antique-filled *hacienda*, 30 minutes' drive from Quito. Ten spacious, beautiful suites have log fires, and Centro Histórico tours, horse riding, cycling, tennis and golf are offered. Reservations only, all-inclusive.
Vía Amaguaña, Quito.
Tel: (02) 233 1632. www. hacienda-ecuador.com

EATING OUT

Café Tianguez ★
Ecuadorian lunch specialities in stunning Plaza de San Francisco.
Tel: (02) 295 4326.
www.sinchisacha.org.
Open: 8am–8pm.

Magic Bean ★
A central, popular place, famous for its breakfasts – locals and tourists alike can get a fix of American food in generous portions in the Mariscal district.
Calle Foch E5-08 & Juan León Mera.
Tel: (02) 256 6181.
Open: 7am–10pm.

La Belle Epoque ★★
Excellent Ecuadorian lunches served in this wood-panelled French dining room with tapestries and low-lit lamps, overlooking colourful Plaza de la Independencia.
Plaza Hotel, corner of Calle García Moreno N5-16 & Chile.
Tel: (02) 251 0777. www. plazagrandequito.com.
Open: 7.30am–11pm.

Mama Clorinda ★★

A safe, if touristy, place to try a range of traditional Ecuadorian specialities such as *locro* (potato soup) and *cuy* (guinea-pig).
Plaza Foch, Reina Victoria 1144 & Calama.
Tel (02) 254 2523.
Open: daily noon–11pm.

Noé Sushi Bar ★★

Luscious lunchtime Japanese finger food – think octopus with avocado and caviar and cooked salmon 'sushi' – served on fashionable black tables among pinky orange walls in the New Town.
Isabel la Católica N24-827 & Coruña. Tel: (02)322 8146. Open: daily 12.30–11pm.

Octava de Corpus ★★

Atmospheric, with fabulous, eclectic contemporary art, extensive wine cellar and home-cooked food served on three tables. Book ahead.
Calle Junín E2-167, Plaza San Marcos.
Tel: (02) 228 0377.
Open: Mon–Sat 12.30– 11pm, Sun noon–4pm.
Spanish-speaking.

Theatrum ★★

This fire-engine-red theatre restaurant, with opulent bar, serves Mediterranean cuisine such as julienned grouper with pea purée, artichoke ragout and zucchini and herb mushrooms.
2nd floor, Teatro Sucre, Plaza del Teatro.
Tel: (02) 257 1011 & (02) 228 9669.
www.theatrum.com.ec.
Open: Mon–Sat 7.30– 11.30pm.

Zazu ★★★

Japanese food prepared by Peruvian-born chef creates an interesting fusion in one of Quito's hippest restaurants, with low-lit elegant evening ambience in the New Town. An eclectic-tasting menu.
Mariano Aguilera 331 & La Pradera.
Tel: (02) 254 3559.
www.zazuquito.com.
Open: Mon–Fri 12.30– 11.30pm, Sat 7–11.30pm.
Closed: Sun.

ENTERTAINMENT

For cultural events see *www.quitocultura.com,* and for other nightlife listings check out *www.experiencequito.com*

La Boca del Lobo

It's hard to miss the lurid painted façade of this wonderfully kitsch bar-restaurant, with its bohemian vibe, vast Mediterranean fusion menu, great cocktails and live music (*Thur & Fri from 9pm*).
Calama 284 y Reina Victoria, Mariscal.
Tel: (02) 223 4083.
www.bocadelobo.com.
Open: Mon–Sat 5pm– 2am.

Café Mosaico

Inlaid tile tables, open fires and candlelight are found at this bohemian restaurant-bar whose balcony is for sundowners with a stupendous Quito view. Try the meze or excellent cheesecake.
Manuel Samaniego N8-95 & Antepara, Itchimbia.
Tel: (02) 254 2871.
www.cafemosaico.com.ec.
Open: Wed–Mon 11am– 10.30pm, Tue 4–10.30pm.

Jacchigua

Excellent Ecuadorian folklore ballet with dazzling costumes and traditional dances and songs from all over the country, from the hat dance of Saraguro to the

Corpus Christi fiesta. Book through Metropolitan Touring (*www.metropolitan-touring.com*).
Teatro Demetrio Aguilera de la CCE.
Tel: (02) 295 2025 & 099 010 624. www.jacchiguaesecuador.com.
Show: Wed 7.30pm.
Dinner show: Thur 7.30pm.

Ñucanchi Peña

A famous *peña* and a place for live traditional Andean music and dancing.
Avenida Universitaria 496 & Armero.
Tel: (02) 254 096.
Open: Wed–Sat 9am–1am.

Seseribo

Quito's oldest, popular and friendly salsa club with great music, orange walls and seats in alcoves surrounding the floor. Best on Thursdays.
Veintimilla 325 & 12 de Octubre, Edificio El Girón, Subsuelo.
Tel: (02) 256 3598.
Open: Wed–Sat 9pm–3am.
Admission charge includes drinks.

Teatro Nacional Sucre

Built in 1880 and restored in 2000, this opera house

with its crushed red velvet seating is an atmospheric place to take in an inexpensive show (with subtitles).
Calle Manabi N8-131, entrance on Guayaquil & Flores, Plaza del Teatro.
Tel: (02) 257 1011 (reservations).
www.arenapremier.com.
Open: Mon–Fri 12.30–4pm & 7–11.30pm, Sat & Sun 7–11.30pm.
Admission charge.

The Biking Dutchman

Offers an imaginative range of excellent mountain-biking tours including Quito to Mindo.
Foch 714 & Juan León Mera. Tel: (02) 256 8323 & 094 205 349. www.bikingdutchman.com

NORTHERN ANDES
Otavalo area
ACCOMMODATION

Aya Huma Hostel ★

Well-run, 22-room hostel with the atmosphere of an indigenous home beside Peguche's old railroad tracks. Otavaleño bands play on Saturday nights and alternative

therapies are offered.
La Vía del Ferrocarril, Peguche. Tel: (06) 269 0164. www.ayahuma.com

Casa Mojanda ★★

Private adobe cottages with mountain views are just part of the attraction at this family-friendly eco-inn supporting community and conservation projects. It offers Andean music, hot tub and organic food along with plentiful excursions including lake kayaking and ethno-cultural tours.
Apartado 160, Otavalo.
Tel: (02) 224 1509 & 094 400 424.
www.casamojanda.com

Polylepis Lodge ★★

Romantic lodge consisting of seven rustic cabins with wood fires, some with Jacuzzi®, set within rare polylepis forest. A night-time walk with a native guide will bring the myths and magic alive.
Carchi, near El Angel.
Tel: (06) 295 4009 & 098 796 476.
www.polylepislodge.com

Hacienda Cusín ★★★

This 17th-century, professionally run

hacienda 15 minutes' drive from Otavalo market is popular at weekends. There's candlelit dining on organic food, an imposing lounge draped with tapestries and a cosy salmon-pink bar. Individually decorated rooms, some with fireplaces, are spread around a cobbled courtyard and activities range from cycling to rose plantation tours.

Otavalo, Imbabura Province.
Tel: (06) 2918 316.
www.haciendacusin.com

Hacienda Pinsaqui ★★★

This elegant, owner-run *hacienda* in historic gardens was once a textile production centre but now has 30 oversized suites with fireplaces, some with original baths. Simón Bolívar slept in room 1, room 8 is romantic, and there's a self-catering family house as well. Famous for *locra* and other Andean specialities to be eaten accompanied by musicians, Pinsaqui is also known for horse riding.

Panamericana Norte Km5,
San Pablo, Imbabura.
Tel: (06) 294 6116
& 092 972 7652. www.
haciendapinsaqui.com

Hacienda Zuleta ★★★★

This large, 16th-century dairy farm (which produces excellent cheese) run by the descendants of past presidents and nestled in scenic countryside has 100 horses, and some cross-Andalucíans are bred here. Riding past pre-Inca Caranqui earth mounds to a condor rehabilitation project is a highlight, as is touring the *hacienda* and tasting grandma's recipes. Pleasant, average-sized, en-suite rooms (named after family members) have super-comfortable beds, wood-burning stoves and no TVs, and suites are planned for the near future. Sumptuous lounges have log fires, drinks and nibbles.

Angochagua, Imbabura Province.
Tel: (06) 266 2182.
www.zuleta.com

EATING OUT

Hacienda Guachalá ★★

Traditional lunch in one of the country's oldest *haciendas*, accompanied by fascinating family stories involving visits from ex-presidents (*see p41*).

Panamericana Norte Km45, Cayambe.
Tel: (02) 236 3042
& 098 146 681.
www.guachala.com

SPORT AND LEISURE

Ride Andes

This highly professional outfit run by a British resident offers one- to eight-day rides for beginners and experienced riders, staying mostly at *haciendas*, from Otavalo to Cotopaxi (*see pp50–51*). Fixed departures or tailor-made, from family programmes to cattle round-ups.

Tel: 099 738 221.
www.rideandes.com

Runa Tupari

Community-based tour operator offering cultural and active experiences with English-speaking indigenous guides and village homestays around Cotacachi (*see p120*).

Sucre & Quiroga, opposite Plaza de los Ponchos, Otavalo.
Tel: (06) 292 5985

☎ 097 286 756.
www.runatupari.com

NORTHWESTERN ANDES

Accommodation

Bellavista Cloudforest Reserve ★

This rustic reserve of bamboo and other natural materials includes 16 en-suite rooms, among them pie-shaped rooms in the bamboo geodesic dome, with balconies (*see p44*). Aimed at serious birders, packages include three daily guided cloudforest hikes. Horse riding and mountain biking are also offered, along with eco-gourmet food and good service. Wheelchair access.
Km52, Vía Quito–Mindo. Tel: (02) 211 6232, reservations (02) 223 2313. www.bellavistacloudforest. com

The Green Horse Ranch ★

Run by a German woman, this ranch specialises in horse treks exploring the ancient verdant Pululahua Crater where it is based.
Casilla 17-12-602 Quito. Tel: (02) 2374847/

086125433 *(mobile).* www.horseranch.de

Maquipucuna Reserve ★

Successful indigenous community project in arguably Ecuador's most beautiful cloudforest, with a basic but comfortable lodge consisting of double and family rooms (three en-suite), hot showers and electricity (*see p120*). Hammocks on the porch, a bathing pool at the foot of a waterfall nearby and walks with native guides. Bookings through Tropic Journeys in Nature and Andean Travel Company (*see p127*).
Parroquia Nanegal. Tel: (02) 250 7200 ☎ 095 096 666. www.maqui.org

Santa Lucia Cloudforest Lodge ★

Efforts to reach this community-owned, award-winning, rustic bamboo-and-thatch lodge in mainly primary mountainous cloudforest are rewarded with a high bird count and remote community experience (*see p121*). Sleeping 20, its shared bathrooms have hot showers but no

electricity, and the mainly organic meals are eaten by candlelight at night. Native guides lead activities.
Barrio la Delicia, Parroquia Nanegal. Tel: (02) 215 7242. www. santaluciaecuador.com

Satchatamia Lodge and Rainforest Reserve ★

A family-friendly lodge on a 350ha (865-acre) reserve. The birding draw is the umbrella bird – black with a plume over its head. Clean and well run with a swimming pool on site and plenty of activities with its own trails and canopy ride, swimming in the river and visits to waterfalls, it is close to the attractions in Mindo. The new adjoining cabins 11 and 12 have the best view, and double beds.
Km 77.7 on the Quito, Calacali, La Independencia road, Mindo. Tel: (02) 390 0906/907. www.sachatamia.com

El Monte Sustainable Lodge ★★

This private, laid-back eco-lodge in Mindo, with six handmade wood-and-thatch riverside cabanas,

has no hotel sign and is reached by cable car. Run by an ecologically minded couple, it offers outstanding gourmet organic vegetarian meals, a lovely al fresco wooden lounge-cum-dining room and nature and birding trails (some on the property). White-water tubing, swimming in natural pools, waterfalls and other visits are also arranged.
Mindo (Pasaje Chantilly). Tel: (02) 390 0402 & 093 084 675, reservations (02) 255 8881. www.ecuadorcloudforest. com

Tandayapa Lodge ★★
A private reserve with a high bird count. This lodge offers 12 rooms and specialist guides to find elusive birds – aimed at serious birders.
El Condor 0e4-145 & Brasil. Tel: (02) 243 3676. www.tanayapa.com

CENTRAL ANDES
Cotopaxi area
ACCOMMODATION
Hacienda La Alegria ★
Built in 1910, this mustard-painted, 24-room organic dairy farm in *chagra* (Andean cowboy) country focuses on riding (from half-day to nine-day rides), rodeos and trekking, and activities for children, including feeding calves, pet llamas and horse rides. Traditional Ecuadorian specialities served.
Near Aloag, Cotopaxi. Tel: (02) 246 2319 & 099 802 526. www. haciendalaalegria.com

Hacienda La Ciénega ★
Having withstood the earthquakes and eruptions of over 300 years, this historic, manager-run *hacienda* has hosted distinguished guests Simón Bolívar and Alexander von Humboldt, who has a vast, sumptuous suite named after him. Sitting in manicured gardens with a gorgeous chapel, its big, basic rooms are good value and frequented by active travellers.
Lasso, Cotopaxi. Tel: (03) 271 9093/9052 & (02) 254 9126. www. hosterialacienega.com

Hacienda El Porvenir ★–★★
A remote and informal, owner-run, orange-painted adobe farmhouse at 3,600m (11,800ft), below Rumiñahui volcano, offering soft adventure in safe hands in the Cotopaxi National Park. It attracts young couples and families, hosted in nine twin-bedded budget rooms and six en-suite rooms, including the Cotopaxi Suite, with a volcano view through its skylight. No phone or Internet.
Quito office: San Ignacio N27-127 & Gonzáles Suarez. Tel: (02) 223 1806 & 094 980 113. www.volcanoland.com

Black Sheep Inn ★★
A popular, award-winning eco-lodge on the remote Quilotoa Loop run by a well-organised American couple (*see pp62–3*). Western vegetarian food is served and the communal lounge and dining is great for singles and the sociable. En-suite 'arriba' rooms have the best cloudforest views; cute wooden cabins and a bunkhouse line the mountainside. Great hiking, mountain biking and horse riding are

offered. Most people stay for three nights at least. Book ahead.
Chugchilán village, Cotopaxi.
Tel: (03) 281 4587.
www.blacksheepinn.com

Hacienda Hato Verde ★★
This deep-pink pumice-and-wood, owner-run *hacienda* in manicured gardens near Cotopaxi National Park focuses on home-made food and horse riding. Six elegant en-suite rooms in the main house, some with volcano views, have fireplace, wooden ceilings, feather duvets and rainforest showers.
Panamericana Km78, entrance to Mulalo.
Tel: (03) 271 9348. www.haciendahatoverde.com

Hacienda San Agustín de Callo ★★★
This romantic *hacienda*, built on the site of an Inca palace, is run by the charismatic Mignon Plaza, descendant of past presidents (*see p65*). A highlight is dining among pillow-shaped Inca walls, alcoves lit by church candles. Six sumptuous suites, nestled

around a cobbled courtyard, are painted with frescoes and have roll-top baths, roaring fires and Frette linen. Cycling, treks and plenty of excursions offered.
Lasso, Cotopaxi.
Tel: (03) 271 9160 & (02) 290 6157.
www.incahacienda.com

EATING OUT
The best places to eat in the area are the *haciendas*. Most offer lunch. Book ahead.

Chugchucaras Rosita ★
The Latacungan speciality of fried pork, corn and fried banana is served by the fourth generation from its most famous restaurant. Makes a filling lunch.
Panamericana Norte, Avenida Eloy Alfaro 31-226 & Gatazo, Latacunga. Tel: (03) 281 3486. Open: Tue–Sun 10am–7pm.

SPORT AND LEISURE
Tierra del Volcán (Volcanoland)
Soft adventure in the Cotopaxi National Park offered through three *haciendas* (*see pp64–5*). Many horse riders are

beginners, mountain biking is a speciality and Cotopaxi climbs, trekking, bird-watching and canopy rides with rappelling are offered.
San Ignacio N27-127 & Gonzáles Suarez, Quito.
Tel: (02) 223 1806 & 094 980 113.
www.volcanoland.com

Baños
ACCOMMODATION
Casa del Abuelo ★
A family-run B&B in a lovely, yellow-painted colonial-style house, on the quieter street leading to the Piscinas de la Virgen. Offering en-suite double rooms, its breakfast and communal rooms are stuffed full of contemporary art.
Montalvo 10-70 & Rafael Vieira, Baños. Tel: (03) 274 2999/09 9825757 (mobile).
www.darvitur.com

J' El Marques Posada ★
Good-value hostel run by a warm-hearted and hospitable Ecuadorian lady. Offers simple but clean en-suite rooms with brightly painted murals, some with balconies and waterfall views. One block

from the Piscinas de la Virgen at the quiet end of town.

Pasaje V Ibarra & Avenida Montalvo.
Tel: (03) 274 0053.
www.marques.banios.com

Hacienda Manteles ★★

This owner-run *hacienda* with volcano views is nestled in a remote valley 20km (12^1/$_2$ miles) from Baños (*see pp57–8*). Its 35 tasteful rooms have fresh flowers and pottery, wood floors, rainforest showers and fireplaces. Two have king-size beds (a rarity in Ecuador), four have Tungurahua views, and there are family rooms too.

Patate. Tel: 098 715 632, Quito office (02) 252 1068. www.haciendamanteles. com

Hosteria Luna Runtun ★★★

The thrill of Baños' most expensive hotel is sleeping in the foothills of an erupting volcano. Suites have stunning views over Baños. The comprehensive spa offers volcanic ash exfoliation, among 25 other treatments, and

spectacular views from outdoor hot pools perched on the cliff's edge. Its 23 activities range from bird-watching to white-water rafting.

Km6, Caserio Runtun, Baños. Tel: (03) 274 0882. www.lunaruntun.com

EATING OUT

Casa Hood ★

International veggie fare in a bohemian atmosphere, with well-stocked bookshelves supplying ample material for reading over a cappuccino, and films shown most nights at 8pm.

Calle Luis A Martinez, behind Santa María Supermarket, Baños. Tel: (02) 274 2668. Open: Wed–Mon 8am–10.15pm, happy hour 5–7pm.

ENTERTAINMENT

Peña Ananitay

A popular and atmospheric place to hear live folk music, with dancing.

16 Diciembre & Espejo, Baños. Open: 9.30pm–3am.

SPORT AND LEISURE

Cordova Tours

Chiva excursions to the waterfalls (10.30am & 3.30pm), the Ruta de la Canela to Puyo (9.30am), volcano-watching (6pm, 9pm & 11pm) and canyoning offered.

Corner of Maldonado & Espejo. Tel: (03) 274 0923 & 099 654 365. www. cordovatours.banios.com

Riobamba and around

ACCOMMODATION

As a transit town, Riobamba suffers from a lack of good hotels, a slight problem as the Chiva Express train leaves early morning.

Estrella de Chimborazo ★

This pink-and-blue acclimatisation lodge with thatched braid roof sits at 3,960m (13,000ft) on the spot of an ancient *tambo*, below stunning Chimborazo. Owned by famous Ecuadorian climber Marco Cruz, its eight rooms are named after famous climbers and it has a dining room with a fireplace snug. Adventure travellers are offered horse riding, mountain biking and trekking, ranging from exploring the polylepis forest to six days of walking around Chimborazo's base. Full board. Booking ahead is essential.

C/o Expediciones Andinas, Las Abras Km3 on the road to Guano, Riobamba.
Tel: (03) 964 915. www. expediciones-andinas.com

Posada de Estación ★
An unusual, budget option is the old station house – at 3,620m (11,880ft) the highest in Ecuador – on an old Inca trail. Owner Rodrigo is an enthusiastic and interesting host, mountain guide and train specialist. Handicrafts workshop, demonstration Indian house in gardens and pet llamas are all on site. It's close to Riobamba, so good as a base for the Chiva Express.
Urbina. Tel: (03) 294 2215 & 099 694 867.

Hostería Andaluza ★★
This good-value, 15th-century *hacienda*, one of Ecuador's oldest, used to be the region's

administrative centre. Ask for a room in the old part, which, although old-fashioned, has more charm than the new. The place hosts groups, and a bonus is live Andean dinner music.
Panamericana Norte Km16. Tel: (03) 294 9370.

Alta Montaña
Entrepreneurial mountain guide Rodrigo Donoso speaks excellent English, runs climbing trips up Chimborazo, which include seeing the traditional ice-cutters, and a range of imaginative treks.
Avenida Daniel León Borja 35-17 & Uruguay, Riobamba.
Tel: (03) 294 2215 & 099 820 963.

Expediciones Andinas
This highly professional outfit, owned and run by famous Ecuadorian climber Marco Cruz, offers climbing expeditions, the Inca trail and horse riding.
Las Abras Km3, road to Guano, Riobamba.
Tel: (03) 964 915. www. expediciones-andinas.com

SOUTHERN ANDES
Cuenca
ACCOMMODATION
Posada del Angel Hostal ★
A clean and pleasant, well-run colonial-house hotel with a family atmosphere and good food in Cuenca's historic centre.
Bolívar 14-11 & Estévez de Toral, Centro Histórico.
Tel: (07) 284 0695 & (02) 282 1360. www. hostalposadadelangel.com

Posada Ingapirca ★
The only place to stay by the ruins, this white and green-shuttered hotel is characterful and friendly with 20 basic but large, clean rooms. The elegant, pretty restaurant serves Ecuadorian lunches near the ruins.
Calle Larga 693 & Borrero, Canar.
Tel: (07) 282 7401.
www.grupo-santaana.com

Santa Lucia ★★
This charming, 20-room, colonial hotel in the heart of the historic district is a mixture of dark woods and murals and mod cons. Spoiling little touches include chocolates and drinks

delivered early evening, fresh flowers, bathtubs and well-trained, interested staff. Good Italian restaurant.

Antonio Borrero 8-44 & Mariscal Sucre, Cuenca. Tel: (07) 282 8000. www.santaluciahotel.com

Eating out

Raymipampa ★

Ecuadorian and international fare is served in a bright atmosphere under the arcades of Cuenca's new cathedral, overlooking Parque Calderón. There's a queue at lunchtimes, so get here early.

Benigno Malo 8-59, between Sucre & Bolívar. Tel: (07) 282 4169. Open: 8.30am–11pm.

Guajibamba ★★

The place to try the national delicacy – roasted *cuy* (guinea pig) – in an olde-worlde atmosphere. Be warned, it comes still with its head and little feet, as is traditional. Book in advance.

Luis Cordero 12-32 & Sangurima, Cuenca. Tel: (07) 283 1016. Open: Mon–Sat 10am–1.30pm & 3–9pm (until 8pm Sat).

Entertainment

Café Eucalyptus

This American-run, bohemian bar-restaurant has over 50 international tapas, from Pad Thai to jerk chicken, and a dizzying range of drinks. A mix of locals and tourists and nightly live music.

Gran Colombia 9-41 & Benigno Malo. Tel: (07) 284 9157. Open: Tue–Thur & Sun 11am–midnight, Fri–Sat 11am–1am.

Sport and leisure

Terra Diversa

Offers imaginative active day tours from Cuenca, such as hiking in Cajas National Park and horse riding along the Inca trail.

Hermano Miguel 5-42 & H Vázquez, Cuenca. Tel: (07) 282 3782 & 099 204 832. www.terradiversa.com

Loja

Accommodation

Grande Hotel Victoria ★★★

Although most travellers head out of Loja city to stay in its surrounds, the best choice in the city is this recently renovated hotel with its aspirational pillars, soaring lobby and spa with an international feel. It offers clean, comfortable rooms and good service in the historic centre, conveniently next to the Biotours office for organising excursions into the surrounding countryside.

Bernardo Valdivieso 0650 & Jose A Eguiguren. Tel: (07) 258 3500. www.grandvictoriabh.com

Vilcabamba

Accommodation

Madre Tierra ★★

This bohemian, homely hotel offers spa treatments and gourmet organic cuisine. Twenty romantic rooms are individually designed in eclectic styles, with frescoes, ambitious bathrooms and some with balconies overlooking gardens filled with birdsong. Visits to the elderly, horse riding to Podocarpus and mountain-trekking can be arranged.

Vilcabamba, Loja. Tel: (07) 264 0269

& 094 465 073.
www.madretierra1.com

Asociación de Guías Nativos de Vilcabamba
An interesting selection of reasonably priced adventure and nature tours is on offer. They also have a few guides who speak English.
Tel: (07) 264 0295 & 094 297 353.
Email: embeflo@yahoo.com
Biotours
Reliable tour operator based in Loja, specialising in southern Ecuador.
Bernardo Valdivieso 0650 and José A E Eguiguren (next to Grand Victoria Hotel).
Tel: (07) 257 9387 & 097 412 909. www. ecuadorsur.com

Zamora
ACCOMMODATION
Copalinga ★
Six wooden, comfortable cabins for two are nestled in a bird-filled cloudforest with trails just 3km (2 miles) from Podocarpus National Park. It's Belgian-run, and birding is a speciality. Home-cooked

meals are also served. Be sure to book well ahead.
Bombuscaro, Zamora.
Tel: 093 477 013.
www.copalinga.com

Zaruma
ACCOMMODATION
Hotel Roland ★
The best of the few places to stay in Zaruma, with comfortable rooms, some with a good view up the valley, and a swimming pool.
Avenida Alonso de Mercadillo, Zaruma.
Tel: (07) 297 2800.

NORTHERN AMAZON
ACCOMMODATION
Termas de Papallacta ★★
Basic but pleasant en-suite rooms in thatched wooden cabins surround shared thermal springs in this tranquil lush green valley at the Amazon's edge (*see pp80–81*). Private Andean-style family cabins with fireplaces are also offered and visited by hummingbirds. The excellent, well-priced spa offers private pools, and treatments include an Andean mud body wrap. The varied restaurant

menu has trout, lamb chops and crêpes suzette. Walks, treks and mountain biking are also on offer. It's full of Quiteños at weekends, so book in advance.
Km67, Vía Quito–Baeza, Papallacta.
Tel: (06) 232 0620 & (02) 256 8989.
www.papallacta.com.ec
Yachana Lodge ★★
Winning *Conde Nast Traveler's* Ecotourism Award in 2004, community development, solar power, organic food and rainforest protection are top priorities at this eco-educational lodge (*see p119*). Yachana has 14 comfortable, if rustic, doubles and four family cabins with hot water and ceiling fans and knowledgeable naturalist guides. A butterfly farm on site and visits to traditional healers are also offered.
Near Mondaña. Quito office: Vicente Solano E1261 & Avenida Oriental.
Tel: (02) 252 3777.
www.yachana.com

Jungle Discovery ★★★

This beautiful cedar boat sailing through the Reserva Faunística Cuyabeno has 15 cabins, the most romantic on the bow with surround windows and an al fresco lounge (*see p84*). It's efficiently run (although cuisine is not a strong point), and the scenery and tranquillity are worth the day to get here. Highlights are meeting the Cofán community and spying pink freshwater dolphins.

Kempery Tours, Ramírez Dávalos 117 y Avenida Amazonas, Oficina 101, Quito. Tel: (02) 222 6583 & 099 551 260.
www.kempery.com

Manatee Amazon Explorer ★★★

This well-established and popular converted river barge plying the Río Napo has 15 spacious cabins, with wooden furniture and a dining deck, and a naturalist guide on board (*see p84*). The itinerary takes in highlights of the area, including a parrot clay-lick, birds and monkeys and an observation tower.

Advantage Travel, El Telégrafo E10-63 & Juan Alcántara, Quito.
Tel: (02) 246 2871. www. manateeamazonexplorer. com

Napo Wildlife Center ★★★

The centre comprises ten cabins at the edge of a blackwater lake frequented by a family of giant sea otters (*see p78*). Ninety minutes by dugout canoe from the Río Napo, this romantic community-owned lodge is one of the best for wildlife, with two parrot clay-licks and a 36m (118ft) canopy observation tower. Relaxed yet intimate – food is served rather than buffet-style – it's ideal for couples and very popular, so book well ahead.

Laguna Anañgu. Quito office: Pinto E4-221 & Avenida Amazonas.
Tel: (02) 255 6348. www. napowildlifecenter.com

Sacha Lodge ★★★

This well-organised, comfortable, Swiss-run lodge in a primary-rainforest private reserve is best known for its dizzying and impressive 275m-long (900ft) canopy walk, 30m (98ft) above the ground. It offers swimming in the lake as well as regular lodge activities. With room for 50 guests and fairly easy access – two and a half hours from Coca by motorised canoe – it tends to attract mature groups and first-timers.

Laguna Pilchicocha. Quito office: Julio Zaldumbide E-14 & Valladolid.
Tel: (02) 256 6090 & 093 778 819.
www.sachalodge.com

Sani Lodge ★★★

This lodge is a circle of ten simple thatched cabins around a lawn in 364sq km (141sq miles) of territory. Community-owned and solar-powered, it's about three or four hours from Coca, has good bird- and animal-watching and a 30m-high (98ft) canopy observation tower.

Laguna Challuacocha. Quito office: Roca E4-49 & Avenida Amazonas (Pasaje Chantilly).
Tel: (02) 025 5888 & 094 341 728.
www.sanilodge.com

Sport and leisure

Ríos Ecuador

Recommended white-water rafting operator, catering for beginners, advanced, and everyone in between. Kayaking also available.

Tarqui 230 & Días de Pineda, Tena.
Tel: (06) 288 6727.
www.riosecuador.com

SOUTHERN AMAZON

Accommodation

Huaorani Ecolodge ★★★

This small, solar-powered, joint-venture eco-lodge is the newest to open in the jungle, and has good eco-credentials (*see p81*). Five secluded bamboo-and-thatch cabins are set along the riverbank with flush toilets and hot showers, and a rich and intimate cultural experience is offered with the semi-traditional Huaorani. Expect jungle walks, traditions such as the blowpipe, dugout canoe rides, a night's camping and 'toxic tour', to witness the damage caused by oil companies.

Near Quehueri'ono Community, Shiripuno River. C/o Tropic Journeys in Nature, La Niña 327 y Reina Victoria.
Tel: (02) 223 4594.
www.huaorani.com

Kapawi Lodge ★★★★

It's the remote location (two weeks' walk to the nearest large town), combined with the cultural experience with the warrior-like Achuar people, that makes this lodge special (*see p81*). It's the most luxurious of the lodges, with polished wood floors and great food. Solar-powered, it has 20 double thatched cabins with hot showers and has been community-owned since 1 January 2008.

Río Pastaza. C/o Complejo Ecoturistíco Kapawi S.A., Edificio Reina Victoria, Piso 1 Oficina 2, Mariscal Foch E7-38 & Reina Victoria, Quito.
Tel: (02) 600 9333.
www.kapawi.com

PACIFIC COAST

Guayaquil

Accommodation

Hotel Las Peñas ★★

Conveniently located near the tourist district, rooms in this good-value, chain-style hotel are spacious, with mod cons. Inner rooms are quiet. There's a handy bakery below.

Escobedo 1215, between Avenida 9 de Octubre & Vélez. Tel: (04) 232 3355.
www.hlpgye.com

Hotel Oro Verde ★★★

This glitzy, large 'Leading Hotel of the World' is the city's best. A huge marble lobby gives way to rather business-like but comfortable rooms, with all the mod cons and a spa, gym and numerous restaurants. The tourist district is in walking distance, the airport close by and the city's best restaurants just paces away.

9 de Octubre & García Moreno, Guayaquil.
Tel: (04) 232 7999. www. oroverdeguayaquil.com

Eating out

Outside hotels, good places to eat in Guayaquil are thin on the ground. Victor Emilio (VE) Estrada in the Urdesa district has international restaurants from Mexican to Italian.

Lo Nuestro ★★

Excellent Ecuadorian food served with finesse

in this traditional, old-style restaurant. Crab is a favourite in Guayaquil.
V E Estrada 903 & Higueras.
Tel: (04) 238 6398.
Open: Mon–Thur noon–3.30pm & 7pm–midnight, Fri–Sun noon–midnight.

El Caracol Azul ★★★
Seafood is a speciality in this celebrated gourmet restaurant with local flair.
9 de Octubre 1918 & Los Ríos.
Tel: (04) 228 0461.
www.elcaracolazul.com.
Open: daily from noon.

ENTERTAINMENT
El Manantial
Inexpensive beer, seafood snacks and live Ecuadorian music nightly.
V E Estrada 520 & Las Monjas, Urdesa, Guayaquil.

Quimbita
Popular bohemian-style indigenous art gallery-cum-sports bar.
Diego Noboa 106 Escalinata 027, Cerro Santa Ana.
Tel: (04) 231 0785.
www.quimbita.com

Guayaquil to Manta
ACCOMMODATION
Alándaluz Tourist Ecological Center ★
Informal, good-value, beachside eco-lodge with 20 bio-cabins, some with turrets under thatch resembling fairy-tale castles, and equally cute inside. Seafood specialities such as *encocado* are served in coconut or bamboo, and drinks are served out of hand-painted pottery goblets. A good base for the area's attractions, it also offers ziplines, horse riding and bird-watching in its own nature park. Swimming in the sea is not advised, but there's a pool.
Puerto Rico, Km12 Puerto López. Tel: (04) 278 0686.
www.alandaluzhosteria.com

El Faro Escandinavo ('The Scandinavian Lighthouse') ★
Nestled beneath the majestic Cape of San Lorenzo, this, the only boutique hotel on the coast, is a haven of elegance, with Norwegian-imported interiors, eight spotless contemporary rooms with glass-tiled showers, classical music and original art. There's beachside dining and a swimming pool in summer. It offers whale- and bird-watching from its windows or from the lighthouse out front, strolls to Panama hat-makers, and walks to howler monkeys.
San Lorenzo, near Manta.
Tel: (09) 112 2336. www.elfaroescandinavo.com

Mantaraya Lodge ★
Brightly painted cave-like curves characterise this adobe lodge within easy access of the Machalilla National Park. More expensive than the Alándaluz, the nice swimming pool, forested view, great service (with waiters in waistcoats) and well-run excursions, including kayaking and horse riding, make up for the noisier, and slightly damp, rooms.
Coast Rd, 3.5km (2 1/4 miles) south of Puerto López. Tel: (09) 404 4050.
www.mantarayalodge.com

EATING OUT
Carmita ★
Seafood specialities (including lobster

ceviche) are served in this long-established, unpretentious restaurant near the beach.
Malecón Julio Izurieta & General Córdova, Puerto López. Tel: (05) 230 0149. Open: daily 8.30am–11pm.

ENTERTAINMENT
Funky Monkey
The most famous bar in this coastal party town, with circular lampshades and white faux leather stools giving it a 70s feel.
Guido Chiriboga & 10 de Agosto, Montañita. Email: Francisco_averos@ hotmail.com

SPORT AND LEISURE
Excursions
Cercapez (*Tel: (05) 230 0173*), **Machalilla Tours** (*Tel: (05) 230 0234*) and **Exploramar** (*Tel: (05) 230 0123*) are reliable tour agencies offering whale-watching excursions, trips to Isla de la Plata and coastal adventure.
General Cordova, Puerto López.

Surfing
In Montañita, surfing packages are arranged from **Casa del Sol**

surfers' hostel
(*Tel: (05) 262 4784. www.casadelsol.com*).
For more casual surfboard hire, try **Tiki Limbo** on the Malecón, before the main intersection to the beach. In Canoa, call **Mark** (*Tel: 092 877 719*) or find him through **Hostal Coco Loco** (*Malecón, Canoa. Tel: 093 972 884*).

Bahía and around
ACCOMMODATION
Bambu ★
A funky bamboo façade in a quiet spot on the beach at the edge of Canoa, with great food and a chilled-out vibe. Rustic rooms with bamboo beds, some en-suite with private balconies, are named after South American countries. Book in advance.
Malecón, Canoa. Tel: (05) 261 6370. www. hotelbambuecuador.com
Chirije ★
Three pleasant, clean and spacious laurel solar-powered cabinas (sleeping 20) in a remote archaeological site backed by dry forest (*see p93*).

Plans are afoot to make these more upmarket to match the beauty of the location, on a long stretch of beautiful, flat-sand, swimming beach, where only the scuttle of crabs and the sound of the wind are heard.
30-minute drive from Bahía de Caráquez. Tel: (05) 269 2008 & 098 120 304.
Casa Grande ★★
Luxurious, boutique-style B&B in an Ecuadorian family home, run by a Spanish-speaking *grande dame* in a quiet location just paces from the seaside Malecón. It has a small swimming pool too.
Casilla 25, Bahía de Caráquez. Tel: 098 120 304.

EATING OUT
Café Flor ★
Lovely, home-cooked, eclectic food and the best breakfast in town, with some outdoor tables.
Central Canoa. Tel: (08) 695 9928. Open: 8.30am–11.30pm.
Seahorse ★★
A surprisingly good organic nouvelle-Ecuadorian restaurant

with wonderful seafood, a few blocks away from the Malecón.

Padre Laennen & C Intriago, Cuidadela Norte, Bahía de Caráquez.
Tel: (05) 269 0187.
Open: Tue–Sun 5–10pm.

ENTERTAINMENT

Hostal Coco Loco
This friendly hangout attracts a fun crowd.
Malecón, Canoa.
Tel: 093 972 884.
Open: daily, until late.

SPORT AND LEISURE

Hostal Coco Loco
This hostel hires surfboards and mountain bikes and offers paragliding with an American (*www.flycanoa.com*) to non-residents.
Malecón, Canoa.
Tel: 093 972 884.

Juliana Cedeno
Helpful and speaking excellent English, Juliana arranges excursions around Bahía, to her property Chirije (*see listing opposite*) and to the mangrove Isla Corazón ('Heart Island').
Tel: (05) 269 2008 & 098 120 304.

GALÁPAGOS ISLANDS
Boat touring
ACCOMMODATION

Eric, Flamingo and Letty ★★★★
These SmartVoyager-certified motor yachts each hold 20 passengers, serve good food and offer a friendly, small-group experience.
Ecoventura, Almagro N31-80 Edificio Venecia, Quito.
Tel: (02) 321 034.
www.ecoventura.com

Isabela II ★★★★
Known for its fine dining and excellent naturalist guides, this romantic luxury yacht with a capacity for 40 even has a Jacuzzi® on deck. Moored at Baltra.
Metropolitan Touring, Avenida de las Palmeras N45-74 & de las Orquídeas, Quito.
Tel: (02) 298 8200.
www.metropolitan-touring.com

La Pinta ★★★★
Launched March 2008, the islands' most luxurious, 63m (207ft) yacht carries 48 passengers. Plush cabins with large windows and a library, Sky Bar, Jacuzzi® and exercise room. Moored at Baltra.
Metropolitan Touring, Avenida de las Palmeras N45-74 & de las Orquídeas, Quito.
Tel: 9020 298 8200.
www.metropolitan-touring.com

Santa Cruz
ACCOMMODATION

Galápagos Safari Camp ★★★
New in 2008, and a first for Ecuador, eight luxury African-style eco-tents with balcony, hot showers and flush toilets sit on a 55ha (136-acre) farm where giant tortoises roam in the highlands. Half an hour's drive from Puerto Ayora.
Highlands, Santa Cruz.
Tel: 091 794 259. www. galapagossafaricamp.com

The Finch Bay Hotel ★★★★
This airy, friendly and chilled eco-hotel, complete with green-painted wooden shutters is tucked across the bay from Puerto Ayora. SmartVoyager-certified, it's the only hotel with its own yacht, and offers island-hopping packages

and 21 lovely, comfortable rooms reached by wooden walkways. The bar and restaurant overlook the sea, and an al fresco Jacuzzi® sits on a private terrace. It also offers mountain bikes, dive packages and, from 2009, spa treatments. Book through Metropolitan Touring (*see p171*).
Puerto Ayora.
Tel: (05) 252 6297.
www.finchbayhotel.com

EATING OUT
William ★
Try coastal specialities such as *encocado* (seafood cooked in coconut sauce) and langostine in the most famous of this row of eateries, recognisable by its murals.
Calle de los Kioskos, Puerto Ayora. Open: 7.30pm–late. Closed: Mon.

Angermeyer Point Restaurant ★★
This restored 1950s building has its own colony of marine iguanas, accessed by water taxi, and is the best restaurant in town, serving seafood specialities.
Punta Estrada, Puerto Ayora. Tel: (05) 252 7007.

www.angermeyerpoint. com. Open: daily for lunch and dinner.

The Rock ★★
The hippest place in town, serving food and cocktails.
Avenida Charles Darwin & Islas Plazas, Puerto Ayora. Tel: (05) 252 7505 & 097 124 934.
Open: noon–11pm.

ENTERTAINMENT
El Bongo
Chilled-out bar attracting tourists and locals with candlelit balcony and pool table inside. Above **La Panga**, the town's disco.
Avenida Charles Darwin between 12 de Febrero & Tomás de Berlanga, Puerto Ayora. Tel: (05) 252 6264. Open: until 2am.

SPORT AND LEISURE
Albatros tours
Snorkelling, daily tours to offshore islands (South Plaza, North Seymour, Bartolomé and Santa Fé, and Floreana). Horse riding, mountain biking and visits to lava tunnels.
Avenida Charles Darwin. Tel: (05) 252 6948 & 084 759 480. www. albatrostoursgalapagos. com. Open: 7am–8pm.

Isabela
ACCOMMODATION AND EATING OUT
The Albemarle ★★★
This elegant but chilled Mediterranean-style hotel is the island's newest. Bright and airy with wood features, its luxurious rooms have marble bathrooms and king-size beds. Its intimate restaurant is the best in town.
Malecón, Puerto Villamil. Tel: (05) 252 9489.
www.hotelalbemarle.com. Restaurant open: 7–9am, noon–2pm & 6–10pm.

SPORT AND LEISURE
Bazar Veronica
Inexpensive cycle hire from this family-run business.
Avenida Antonio Gil (opposite National Parks office). Tel: (05) 252 9116.
Tropic Journeys in Nature
This ecotourism specialist offers an active Isabela tour (*see p109*).
Avenida República E7-320 y Almagro. Edificio Taurus Departimento 1-A, Quito. Tel: (02) 222 5907 & (02) 223 4594.
www.tropiceco.com

Index

Acknowledgements

Thomas Cook wishes to thank NICKI GRIHAULT for the loan of the photographs reproduced in this book, to whom the copyright in the photographs belongs, except the following:

COPALINGA 9
DREAMSTIME.COM 57 (Ryszard Laskowski), 85 (Asdf_1), 90 (Robert Lerich)
FONDO MIXTO 18, 61, 69
NHPA/PHOTOSHOT 40
PHOTO BANK METROPOLITAN TOURING/ECUADOR 126 (Francisco Montesdeoca), 143 (Luis Guzman)
WIKIMEDIA COMMONS 73 (Delphine Ménard), 121 (Jack Alvis Ratcliffe)
WORLD PICTURES/PHOTOSHOT 100

For CAMBRIDGE PUBLISHING MANAGEMENT LTD:
Project editors: Karen Beaulah & Robert Wilkinson
Typesetter: Paul Queripel
Copy editor: Anne McGregor
Proofreader: Jan McCann
Indexer: Karolin Thomas

The author would like to give particular thanks to Dominic Hamilton at the Quito Visitor Bureau (QVB) without which this guide wouldn't have been possible, Rosario Arroyo, Metropolitan Touring (MT), London office, who believed in it, and Tamara Karolys and Sylvia Moncayo, for their support on the ground. Special thanks also to Alfonso Tandazo of Surtrek, Jascivan Carvalho of Tropic Journeys in Nature and Bram van Leeuwen of Andean Travel Company. Thanks to my guides and other staff who went out of their way to help – kind Ecuadorian people.

For contacts and information, particular thanks to Think Galapagos, the Latin America Tourism Association (LATA), Simon Heyes of Senderos and Patricio Tamariz, director of the Fondo Mixto (Ministry of Tourism). Thanks also to Tim Murray Walker of Journey Latin America (JLA); Stephen Bray of Bales Worldwide; Julie Middleton of Trips Worldwide and Sue Ockwell, representing Sunvil Latin America. For photographic assistance, thanks to Bayeux, London and Jeremy and Chizuko Hoare.

SEND YOUR THOUGHTS TO
BOOKS@THOMASCOOK.COM

We're committed to providing the very best up-to-date information in our travel guides and constantly strive to make them as useful as they can be. You can help us to improve future editions by letting us have your feedback. If you've made a wonderful discovery on your travels that we don't already feature, if you'd like to inform us about recent changes to anything that we do include, or if you simply want to let us know your thoughts about this guidebook and how we can make it even better – we'd love to hear from you.

Send us ideas, discoveries and recommendations today and then look out for your valuable input in the next edition of this title.

Emails to the above address, or letters to Travellers Series Editor, Thomas Cook Publishing, PO Box 227, Unit 9, Coningsby Road, Peterborough PE3 8SB, UK.

Please don't forget to let us know which title your feedback refers to!